The blue lotus The blue lotus The blue lotus
The blue lotus The blue lotus The lotus
The blue lotus The
blue The lotus The
lotus The
blue

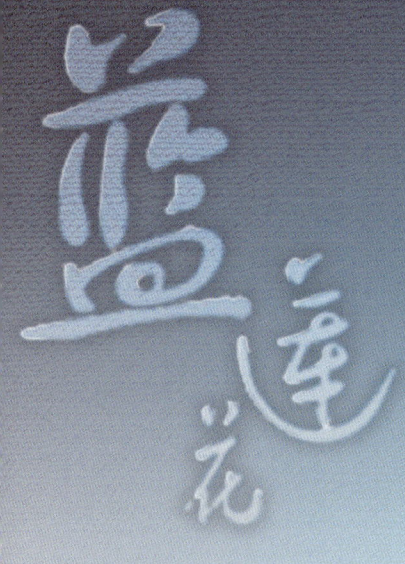

歌词英译·杂谈

李杜 著

武汉大学出版社

图书在版编目(CIP)数据

蓝莲花：歌词英译·杂谈/李杜著.—武汉：武汉大学出版社,2009.9
　ISBN 978-7-307-07047-9

　Ⅰ.蓝…　Ⅱ.李…　Ⅲ.①歌词—英语—翻译　②随笔—作品集—中国—当代　Ⅳ.H315.9　I267.1

中国版本图书馆 CIP 数据核字(2009)第 133370 号

责任编辑：郭园园

出版发行：武汉大学出版社　（430072　武昌　珞珈山）
　　　　　（电子邮件：cbs22@whu.edu.cn　网址：www.wdp.com.cn）
印刷：湖北恒泰印务有限公司
开本：787×1092　1/16　　印张：6.75　字数：65 千字　插页：1
版次：2009 年 9 月第 1 版　　2009 年 9 月第 1 次印刷
ISBN 978-7-307-07047-9/H·664　　定价：26.00 元

版权所有，不得翻印；凡购我社的图书，如有缺页、倒页、脱页等质量问题，请与当地图书销售部门联系调换。

前言

  我开始翻译流行歌词，是在新东方的课堂。有位男生，想给心仪已久的女生送一句话，"我能想到的最浪漫的事，是和你一起慢慢变老。"求我译成英文，以迎合其风雅。

  我正在强调介词短语的重要性，苦口婆心。于是拿句子里的"慢慢"举例。要体现其天长地久，莫过于用一组介词短语，"hour by hour, year by year, and millennium by millennium"。当时还故作玄虚，宣称这三个词 hour, year, 和 millennium 发音都是颤音，符合心悸与忐忑的情境，这样，语义与发音天人合一。举座哗然，同时深有所悟。

  从此便一发不可收拾。我翻译歌词，纯粹是个人化的翻译，往往兴之所至，只为把玩文字，不求文体符合，更无从跟随原曲吟唱。只因其贴近学生的情感与生活，在英语教学上却另辟蹊径，自己也沉溺其中，自得其乐。

  承蒙武大出版社郭圆圆老师青睐，敦促我结集出版。自己觉得文字鄙陋，难登大雅之堂。后来思忖，不经过大方之家贻笑一番，何来进步？便草草收集几曲，呈送读者，细细摆在面前，自己缩手耸肩，低眉垂目，等待英语同好们随意翻捡，评头论足。

李杜
2009年7月

CONTENTS 目录

月亮代表我的心 4
THE MOON SPEAKS OF MY MIND

大约在冬季 8
POSSIBLY IN WINTER

女人花 16
WOMAN OF FLOWER

橄榄树 20
THE OLIVE TREE

蓝莲花 40
THE BLUE LOTUS

怒放的生命 44
LIFE IN BURSTING BLOOM

生死不离 60
DEATH WON'T DO US PART

笔记 65
A RECORDED MEMORY

乘客 69
THE PASSENGER

穿过你的黑发的我的手 13
WHEN MY HAND RAN THROUGH YOUR HAIR

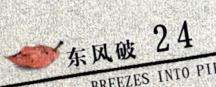
东风破 24
BREEZES INTO PIECES

发如雪 28
HAIR FLOWING SNOW FALLING

花田错 31
ERROR UPON ERROR

谁动了我的琴弦 35
WHO PLUCKED MY STRINGS

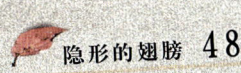
隐形的翅膀 48
WINGS INVISIBLE

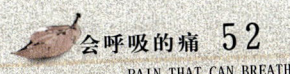
会呼吸的痛 52
PAIN THAT CAN BREATHE

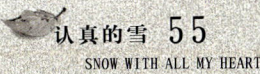
认真的雪 55
SNOW WITH ALL MY HEART

一千年以后 74
IN A THOUSAND YEARS

杂 谈

- 几句武侠英译 ———————————— 78
- 一段武汉话英译 ———————————— 80
- 武汉话"你嚇我"的英译 ———————— 82
- 我和谁都不争 ———————————— 84
- 麦秋已过 ——————————————— 86
- 关于博客 ——————————————— 88
- 一首戏谑的英文诗 —————————— 90
- 吴宓翻译的一首英文诗 ———————— 92
- 英国人和美国人 ———————————— 94
- 为了坠落的飞翔 ———————————— 96
- 赵承熙枪击案一：心是孤独的猎手 —— 98
- 赵承熙枪击案二：更多的人死于心碎 —— 100
- 70年前对失利奥运健儿的鼓励 ———— 102

月亮代表我的心

The moon speaks of my mind

孙仪（词）

你问我爱你有多深
You ask me how deep my love shall grow;

我爱你有几分
And how much I care for you.

我的情也真
All my care is real;

我的爱也真
All my love is blind;

月亮代表我的心
The moon speaks of my mind.

你问我爱你有多深
You ask me how deep my love shall grow;

我爱你有几分
And how much I care for you.

我的情不移
My heart shall never change;

我的爱不变
By you I shall always stand;

月亮代表我的心
The moon speaks of my mind.

轻轻的一个吻
Nothing but a tender kiss,

已经打动我的心
And my heart's melted away;

深深的一段情
Nothing but a loving story,

叫我思念到如今
And I've pined for you to this day.

你问我爱你有多深
You ask me how deep my love shall grow;

我爱你有几分
And how much I care for you.

你去想一想
Go and think for a while,

你去看一看
Go and gaze for a while,

月亮代表我的心
The moon speaks of my mind.

月亮

论及流行歌曲,《月亮代表我的心》堪称代表作。曲风温婉,歌词简洁。邓丽君唱得缠绵缱绻。在我耳边萦绕的,却是齐秦的版本,带着男性的婉转深情。

那年在剑桥小镇的酒吧里,窗外明月高悬,我受命带着同事们低吟浅唱《月亮代表我的心》,作为背景音乐;同时,牛高马大的犹太人Joe,梳着油光可鉴的大背头,摇头晃脑,用英文朗诵徐志摩的《再别康桥》。周边英国人,微笑着侧目而视,不懂这群人在演绎何种深情。

招待我们这一桌的小男孩,极其殷勤可亲,17岁,来自葡萄牙。我素不喜半熟的牛排,便施展刀工,细细削下表面的熟肉,大快朵颐后,只剩下盘子上血糊拉滋的一坨。小招待远远瞥见,目瞪口呆。

听说我们是中国人,小招待自告奋勇,要演示一句中文,却因首次汇报演出,紧张之下,一时语塞。一阵抓耳挠腮后,表情骤然灿烂。我们停下刀叉,静静等待。听得小招待兴冲冲地说:"撒哟那拉,撒哟那拉。"举座哗然。我本以为小招待孺子可教,想为他讲讲庖丁解牛、游刃有余之类的风情,如今看到他脸上亢奋冲动的青春痘,只得悻悻作罢。

回到这首歌。我翻译歌词,往往兴之所至,只为把玩文字,不求文体符合。《月亮代表我的心》,歌词简易通顺,反而不好把握。此番我却持了严谨的态度,尽量遵循歌词翻译的原则,让英文也能配上曲调,朗朗上口。

月亮代表我的心

"月亮代表我的心"这句话,"心"应该为"心思"之意,译成"heart"似乎不妥。"代表"如译成"represent",会流于生硬。用"speak of one's mind"这一短语,符合原文浅显直白的风格。

在西方文化里,文人骚客对月亮却熟视无睹,并不热衷。描述月亮,仅仅就事论事,与一诉衷肠相去甚远。不过,读过拜伦的一首诗:

Art thou pale for weariness
    Of climbing heaven and gazing on the earth,
Wandering companionless
    Among the stars that have a different birth,
And ever changing, like a Joyless eye
    That finds no object worth its constancy?

难得拜伦如此细腻,一反《西风颂》的豪情。"月亮,你游走天穹,俯瞰大地,疲惫不堪,面色苍白,与群星格格不入,像一只毫无生趣而善变的眼睛,阴晴圆缺。难道世上万物,都不值得你的专一?"

殊途同归。拜伦笔下的月亮,不也speaks of my mind么?

大约在冬季

POSSIBLY IN WINTER

齐秦（词）

轻轻地我将离开你
Quietly I am taking my leave,

请将眼角的泪拭去
Please wipe away your tears.

漫漫长夜里未来日子里
In endless nights of the days to come,

亲爱的你别为我哭泣
My love, shed no tears and be strong.

前方的路虽然太凄迷
The road ahead is gloomy enough,

请在笑容里为我祝福
Yet smile a blissful smile in my behalf.

虽然迎着风虽然下着雨
Despite all the wind and rain I shall stand.

我在风雨之中念着你
In whatever storm you are always on my mind.

没有你的日子里
Since you are not around,

我会更加珍惜自己
I'll make each and every day count.

没有我的岁月里
In the days without me,

你要保重你自己
My love, careful as can be!

你问我何时归故里
"When will you return home?" you asked,

我也轻声地问自己
While in my ears the same question was cast.

不是在此时不知在何时
Not this moment is all I know,

我想大约会是在冬季
Possibly in winter when it shall snow!

不是在此时不知在何时
Not this moment is all I know,

我想大约会是在冬季
Possibly in winter when it shall snow!

"当君怀归日,是妾断肠时"

在我们70后眼里,《大约在冬季》的年代,与青涩、萌动、惆怅重重叠叠。似乎是1986年左右,我上初二,磁带封面上的齐秦,一袭紧身黑衣,蓬头细腿,神色冷峻。一曲《大约在冬季》在耳机里缠绵反侧,愁绪漫卷而来,让不知愁的少年拼却一醉。讲台上浮动着数学老师一张一翕的嘴,我面前铺着刚发下的试卷,鲜红的叉叉,鬼魅般影影绰绰。

20多年后的此时,一场倒春寒正席卷南方,武汉从前几天的温煦坠入冰窖。我坐在窗前翻译《大约在冬季》,冷雨飘零,春寒料峭,沉沉的阴霾压下来,催生所有关于冬季的回忆。像艾略特在《荒原》里用反语写道,"Winter kept us warm, covering earth in forgetful snow…"

"大约在冬季"这句敷衍塞责的回答,在翻译上不好处理,用about in winter?还是perhaps in winter?几经踌躇,我选择possibly in winter,加深了不确定性,聊以搪塞归家的追问。

"你问我何时归故里……不是在此时,不知在何时,我想大约会是在冬季。"天涯羁旅,壮志未酬,心有不甘,却系着柔情的牵绊。漫不经心的回答,尽藏无奈。切切的女子,执迷不悟,不求荣华富贵,惟愿终日厮守,哪管春夏秋冬?

李白有一首《春思》,"当君怀归日,是妾断肠时。"翻成英文如下:
At long last you think of returning home
The moment my heart is nearly broken.

可否当作含混答案—— possibly in winter ——的凄恻回复?

穿过你的黑发的我的手

WHEN MY HAND RAN THROUGH YOUR HAIR

罗大佑（词）

穿过你的黑发的我的手
When my hand ran through your hair,

穿过你的心情的我的眼
And when my eyes see through your mind,

如此这般的深情若飘逝转眼成云烟
In a blink of an eye a deep love went into the air

搞不懂为什么沧海会变成桑田
As an ocean turning into fields by a magic hand.

牵着我无助双手的你的手
When helpless I longed for your hands to hold

照亮我灰暗双眼的你的眼
and for your glance to light up my gloomy eyes.

如果我们生存的冰冷的世界依然难改变
even if the world we live stayed cruel and cold

至少我还拥有你化解冰雪的容颜
I can still turn to your smile to melt all the ice.

『老 歌』

　　张学友的一首老歌。初听是在中学时代。

　　听老歌的享受，在重温过去。曲调里尘封着当时的人、事、情景，歌声再次响起，以往缓缓展开。

　　实验中学的小操场，梧桐遮天蔽日，记忆里铺着温煦的阳光。食堂，终日浮着陈年油垢的厚重气息，地上零星残留着不慎打翻的饭菜，我们紧紧攥着油腻腻软塌塌的饭票，兴高采烈地挤得满头大汗，唯恐天下不乱。

　　有人奋力挤到小窗口，随口喊道："氽汤圆子，伙计！"里面的胖大婶勃然变色，忿忿把碗磕在窗沿上，雪白的搪瓷片四散开来，一阵唾沫星子也及时赶到。

　　"你姆妈才跟我是伙计！"胖嫂厉声道。

　　操场边，有好学的同学躲在一隅念念有词，树荫下，有少男少女追踪彼此身影的躲闪目光。脸上都映着斑斑驳驳的青春。

　　那时的球星是唐尧东、朱波、傅玉斌，郝海东还是小将。我们啃着6分钱加一两粮票的面窝，读着汪国真、席慕容酸溜溜的儿女情长，心里有三毛环游世界的梦想在疯狂滋长。

　　1985到1991，是我的中学时代。

　　耳边，张学友在低吟浅唱，深情款款。我的记忆，与风月无干。

Flowering Woman

我有花一朵
There is a flower

种在我心中
Growing in my heart,

含苞待放意幽幽
Ever budding in anticipation.

朝朝与暮暮
Each and every dawn or dusk

我切切地等候
I wait on tiptoe for my beloved

有心的人来入梦
Till he steps into my dreams.

女人花
Woman of flower,

摇曳在红尘中
Swaying in the worldly Red Dust,

女人花
Woman of flower,

随风轻轻摆动
Rocking in gentle breezes,

只盼望 有一双温暖手
Is yearning for a hand to stretch out

能抚慰 我内心的寂寞
To warm up my lonely heart.

Flowering Woman

我有花一朵
There is a flower,

花香满枝头
fragrance wafting through branches.

谁来真心寻芳踪
Who comes in earnest for her?

花开不多时啊
She is here today and gone tomorrow.

堪折直须折
Pluck while there is time

女人如花花似梦
for women are flowers, and flowers, dreams.

『 一株开花的树 』 A flowering tree

  关于女人花,我在考虑两种译法。一个是woman of flower,一个是flowering woman。后者让我想起一幕歌剧,"a flowering tree",一株开花的树,与《女人花》异曲同工。那是2006年,作曲家约翰·亚当斯(John Adams)和导演彼得·赛拉斯(Peter Sellars)合作推出一部新歌剧,作为维也纳皇家新希望艺术节的揭幕演出。剧中的空灵和魔幻源于莫扎特the magic flute里的灵感。

  歌剧取材于一个南印度的民间传说。有位穷苦姑娘,擅长施展魔法。每天夜里,把自己变成一株开花的树,花团锦簇。妹妹把花朵摇落,一地缤纷。第二天妹妹去卖花,所得微薄,聊以赡养贫病老母。

  一天夜里,一位王子偷偷看到这一幕。诧异之余,过目难忘,便央求国王父亲,让自己迎娶姑娘。进宫后,王子希望她施展魔法,姑娘不从,受到冷落。姑娘无奈,只得变成一株开花的树。王子欣喜万分。

  不料,这一幕被王子乖戾的妹妹窥见。王子妹妹趁王子外出,带了一群客人,强行让姑娘表演魔法,却在中途感到兴味索然,无趣而散。狂风暴雨中,魔法中断,姑娘化为半人半树,流落街头,被一群吟游诗人收养。

  王子归来后,茶饭不思,潜出皇宫,寻找妻子,最终穷困不堪,沦为乞丐,蓬头垢面。一系列的波折后,王子奄奄一息。他的妹妹听说一帮吟游诗人可以治好王子,便将他们招入宫中,让他们的半人半树怪物唱歌,以曼妙歌声治疗王子的心病。

  故事的结局显而易见。王子和姑娘重逢,悲喜交加。王子打来两桶水,完成了未继的魔法仪式,姑娘回复原样,两人过上幸福的生活。每天夜幕降临,便有一株开花的树,亭亭如盖。

橄榄树

三毛（词）

The olive tree

橄榄树 THE OLIVE TREE

不要问我从哪里来
Ask me not where I am from;

我的故乡在远方
Far, far away is my hometown.

为什么流浪
流浪远方
I know not why I am ever a vagabond
To the horizon and beyond.

为了天空飞翔的小鸟
In search of birds in a free flight,

为了山间轻流的小溪
Streams trickling down the hills,

为了宽阔的草原
And a grassland wide and vast,

流浪远方
I am drifting afar.

还有还有
And above all else,

为了梦中的橄榄树
The olive tree in my dreams.

我这一代人的流浪梦想里,《橄榄树》是一曲永远的怀念,总能漾起当年的青春迷茫气息。

1991年年初,三毛自杀,我读高三,半年后的高考正悄然逼近,阴霾密布,我在忧惧中惶惶不可终日。得知消息后的失落和震荡,至今记忆犹新。

我通读过三毛的文章。后来选择学习语言,隐隐与此相关。她笔下青涩压抑的少年时代,令我心有戚戚。她选择逃学,沉浸在中文文学,杂览闲读的经历,让我看到自己的影子。只是我没有那么叛逆和决绝,仅仅在数学习题集下,暗暗压着一本《收获》,偷偷寻着文字的快乐。

另外,和三毛一样,我在少年时代,也学过美术。父亲后期从事美学研究,曾是省美学学会副会长,当时会长是武大的刘纲纪教授。家里络绎来往的那些长发蓬松、胡茬参差的艺术家,让我耳濡目染。家里订的《文艺研究》、《美育》、《艺术欣赏》等,被我草草翻阅过无数,以打发数理化的百般无聊。

在那个时代，三毛笔下的画面，对我影响至深。流浪的梦想，暗然滋长。家里有一套《各国概况》，上下两册，我读得滚瓜烂熟。尤其是南美和非洲部分。只要提及任何国家，我必能答出其人种构成，以及官方语言是西班牙语、葡萄牙语还是英语。

2009年，有一回和Paul作讲座，Paul谈及在加那利群岛住过4年。我知道英国人Paul娶了西班牙妻子，却不知和 Canary Islands 缘分至深。一刹那，我又看到三毛笔下的沙漠、残阳、蒙着白纱的女子，以及羞涩和善的大胡子渔人。心里掠过寂寞的海风，暮色苍然。

"不要问我从哪里来，我的故乡在远方。"这句话，萦绕着不散的乡愁。英文里有一个词 nostalgia，"乡愁"，在我的记忆里，唱着永远的橄榄树。

東風破

BREEZES INTO PIECES

方文山（词）

一盏离愁孤单伫立在窗口　我在门后假装你人还没走
All alone in wait by the window,
stands a sad lamp in parting sorrow.
To linger behind the unbelieving gate,
Isn't my longing gaze all but too late?

旧地如重游月圆更寂寞　夜半清醒的烛火不忍苛责我
Lonelier is the moon full and cold;
bitter still is when an old love retold.
A midnight candle struggles to keep awake,
Isn't a sleepless grief all but my mistake?

一壶漂泊浪迹天涯难入喉　你走之后酒暖回忆思念瘦
To the end of the world I drift,
With a pot of wine too heavy to lift.
The wine revives a memory thin and thick.
Doesn't it warm up all but a heart so love—sick?

水向东流时间怎么偷　花开就一次成熟我却错过
How can I bear to steal the hour
As water flows east to catch a flower,
Soon blooming, soon withering, and so forgotten.
Didn't my life miss all but a fateful blossom?

谁在用琵琶弹奏一曲东风破　岁月在墙上剥落看见小时候
Who played upon a lute amid eastern breezes,
Heart torn apart and tune falling into pieces?
A weary wall stands peeling and silent.
Doesn't it remind all but an age innocent?

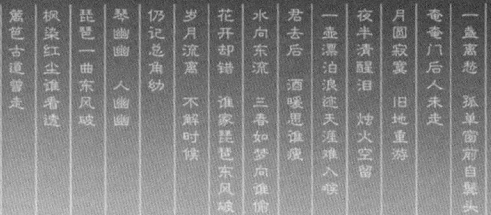

一盏离愁 孤单窗前自鬓头
奄奄门后人未走
月圆寂寞 旧地重游
夜半清醒的烛火 不忍苛责我
一壶漂泊 浪迹天涯难入喉
君去后 酒暖思谁瘦
水向东流 三春如梦向谁偷
花开却错 谁家琵琶东风破
岁月流离 不解时候
仍记总角幼
琴幽幽 人幽幽
琵琶一曲东风破
枫染红尘谁看透
篱笆古道曾走

犹记得那年我们都还很年幼 而如今琴声幽幽我的等候你没听过
Youthful hours are no more and passed.
Am I alone holding to by-gones fast?
In vain is the music blown to float.
Isn't my wait all but a sobbing note?

谁再用琵琶弹奏一曲东风破 枫叶将故事染色结局我看透
Never could the same lute ever play
A tune long gone and blown far away.
Maples live for a moment bright and brief.
Wouldn't our story come to all but a grief?

篱笆外的古道我牵着你走过 荒烟漫草的年头就连分手都很沉默
Beyond hedges an ancient path forgot the time
When we walked along with your hand in mine.
Parting words speak less than a silent tear.
Isn't memory all but smoky grass far and near?

東風破

Breezes into Pieces

一盏离愁　孤单窗前自鯁头
奄奄门后人未走
月圆寂寞　旧地重游
夜半清醒泪　烛火空留

一壶漂泊浪迹天涯难入喉
君去后　酒暖思谁瘦
水向东流　三春如梦向谁偷
花开却错　谁家琵琶东风破

岁月流离　不解时候
仍记总角幼
琴幽幽　人幽幽
琵琶一曲东风破
枫染红尘谁看透
黛烟古道曾走
荒烟漫草年年头
分飞后

东风与西风

我是由《东风破》开始，成了周杰伦的拥趸。全劳方文山先生匠心独具，将白话与古风糅杂，意境玄远，令青年人潜移默化，醉心中华文明，功莫大焉。

我自不量力，把《东风破》译成英语，让英文渗透着中文的古意。方文山将中国古诗字句巧妙组合，创立了似曲牌名的"东风破"，却让我在翻译中大费踌躇。因为在"风"的意境上，中西文化迥然有别。

中国的西风来自西伯利亚，从而"昨夜西风凋碧树"。只有东风暖意融融，"等闲识得东风面，万紫千红总是春"。英国因北大西洋暖流之故，西风乃和暖温润之风。英国诗人John Masefield有一首诗，曰"西风"(the west wind)，首句便是：It's a warm wind, the west wind, full of birds' cries; I never hear the west wind but tears are in my eyes. 大意是："西风拂来，满面温煦，百鸟鸣唱。西风的讯息，令我热泪盈眶。"

《东风破》里，东风与残破叠加，反衬出萧索。这一况味，英文望尘莫及。我只能顾及字形美与音韵美的枝节，译成"breezes into pieces"，差强人意，文化意境早已七零八落。

"谁在用琵琶弹奏一曲东风破"一句，"弹奏琵琶"，我用了合规语法的"play upon a lute"，却心有不甘。若用over替换upon，"play over a lute"，也许不合英语语法，却贴近中国文化意境。介词on或upon指有接触的上面，而over指悬空的上面。弹琵琶，指尖应轻触琴弦，得用"upon"。但在这里，不是手指在弹，而是心之共鸣。纤纤玉指，悬而不弹，一首心曲，早已兀自鸣咽。

只有介词over，才能体现这一风情。为了语法，失了意境，可惜。记得英国诗人叶芝（Yeats）有一句"autumn was over him"，描述"他身上披满秋色"，让我对介词over另眼相看，觉得摇曳多姿，而on, upon, in, at等介词在我眼里，从此生硬难耐，面目可憎。

方文山（词）

Hair Flowing Snow Falling

狼牙月伊人憔悴 我举杯饮尽了风雪
A crescent moon, cold and gray,
Was like my fair lady pining away.
Wine-cup in hand,
I downed snowy wind of all kind.

是谁打翻前世柜 惹尘埃是非
Under whose hand was my former life upset,
Where a dusted love and hate met?

缘字诀几番轮回 你锁眉哭红颜唤不回
Our fate is already written down,
No matter how many times it goes round.
Hard and sad you wrinkle your brows
Crying over beauty fading like the hours.

纵然青史已经成灰我爱不灭
Even if history goes up in ashes
My love never ever dies.

繁华如三千东流水 我只取一瓢爱了解 只恋你化身的蝶
Of all the bustling waters flowing east in thousands
I take only one scoop to bear in our minds,
Obsessed with the butterfly
Flapping in your after life.

你发如雪凄美了离别 我焚香感动了谁
Hair flowing, snow falling,
It takes beauty and sorrow to make a parting.
Whose heart is touched when incenses are burning?

邀明月 让回忆皎洁 爱在月光下完美
Inviting the moon to light up a past,
Full, and bright, the love shall ever last.

你发如雪纷飞了眼泪 我等待苍老了谁
Your hair flows as the snow falls,
Scattering away hot tears.
Who, in my wait, has advanced in years?

红尘醉 微醺的岁月 我用无悔刻永世爱你的碑
Slightly drunken is the worldly Red Dust;
Regret-it-not is the memorial ever carved in my heart.

『独立主格』

　　一曲《发如雪》，寂寥苍凉。首阕里一句"我举杯，饮尽了风雪"，我译成"Wine-cup in hand, I downed snowy wind of all kind."其中down，在这里作动词，一饮而尽，豪迈悲绝。"我举杯"译成"wine-cup in hand"，运用了名词加介词短语的独立主格结构。

　　独立主格结构(the absolute construction)是大学英语语法难点之一，在考试中频频出现。它用于修饰整个句子，作为一种独立结构，而不是一个词或词组。因为用法特殊，学子望而生畏。其实独立主格自有风情万种的一面，它多用于描述性语言，呈现动作或状态，栩栩如生，令人身临其境。

发如雪

『独立主格』

除了以上wine-cup in hand这种名词加介词短语的形式，独立主格结构还常常表现出名词（或主格代词）加分词。如《东风破》中的高潮部分：

谁在用琵琶弹奏一曲东风破，
岁月在墙上剥落看见小时候。
Who played upon a lute amid eastern breezes, heart torn apart and tune falling into pieces? A weary wall stands peeling and silent. Doesn't it remind all but an age innocent?

《东风破》只能直译，还增加了"伤心"一层意思（heart torn apart）。heart torn apart and tune falling into pieces 就是典型的名词加分词的独立主格结构。心被撕裂，被动，用过去分词；曲不成调，主动，用现在分词。一曲琵琶，伤心欲裂，东风残破，岁月凋零。

意味深长，含蓄隽永。这种带分词的独立主格结构也体现在：

你发如雪，凄美了离别，我焚香感动了谁？
Hair flowing, snow falling,
It takes beauty and sorrow to make a parting.
Whose heart is touched when my incense is burning?

把"发如雪"的意境，用独立主格结构"Hair flowing, snow falling"来表达，黑发飘零，雪花披纷，不比直白的"hair is like snow"更富意境吗？

陈镇川（词）

ERROR UPON ERROR

夜好深了　纸窗里怎么亮着
Deep in the night
Why does the paper window still leak light?

那不是彻夜等候　你为我点的烛火
Do you stay up all night
Only to share with me a faint candlelight?

不过是一次邂逅　红楼那一场梦
Nothing but a chance encounter
Or a dream in the Red Chamber.

我的山水全部褪了色　像被大雨洗过
Strips my landscape of all its color
As if washed away by a downpour.

杯中景色鬼魅　忘了我是谁
In my cup shades and shadows flicker;
　"But who I am ?" I wonder.

心情就像夜凉如水　手里握着蝴蝶杯　单飞 不飞不归
An easy mind flows as night falls, cool as water.
I hold a cup printed with a butterfly,
Unpaired, on a homeless flight .

花田里犯了错 说好 破晓前忘掉
Error upon error in a Flower Festival,
Before dawn comes a promise to forget all.

花田里犯了错 拥抱 变成了煎熬
Error upon error in a Flower Festival,
Reducing an embrace into an ordeal.

花田里犯了错 犯错 像迷恋镜花水月的无聊
Error upon error in a Flower Festival,
As vain as a fascination over
Flowers in a mirror and the moon on the river.

花田里犯了错 请 原谅我多情的打扰
Error upon error in a Flower Festival,
Will you take offence for my love-sick role?

醉 怎么会喝醉 美因为你的美
I am so drunk that I can't believe it
Intoxicated by your overwhelming beauty.

爱匆匆一瞥不过点缀飞 看大雪纷飞
Love is but a glance, only meant for a show,
Flowing scattered as the snow.

却再找不回 被白雪覆盖那些青翠
Back I come, yet unable to bring
The snow-covered spring.

当时空成为拥有你唯一条件 我 又醉
When space and time stand in my way
I am dead drunk once again.

琥珀色的月　结成了霜的泪
The moon, amber-colored
Has iced up into tears of frost.

我会记得这段岁月
Freezing this moment to mark a love lost.

Only to和chance

　　花田错源出《水浒》第五回，"小霸王醉入销金帐，花和尚大闹桃花村"。落魄书生卞济卖画为生，与官家小姐刘月英邂逅花田盛会，但小霸王周通从中阻挠，引发一连串危机。人谓：花田盛会，一错再错；千古姻缘，好事多磨。错上加错，英文可以用error upon error。

　　那不是彻夜等候 你为我点的烛火
　　Do you stay up all night
　　Only to share with me a faint candlelight?

　　这一句里的only to 值得一提。我的印象里，永远残存着一个例句："当小明赶到火车站，发现火车已经离开了。"还凑上语法解释，表示惋惜遗憾的情绪云云。这个语法点和例句，如难兄难弟，难舍难分。就像虚拟语气里，少不得会有"如果明天下雨，我们就不开运动会"一句，仿佛终身制的铁饭碗，永不退休。谁愿意去啃这些乏味无聊的语法书？

花田错

记得我在英语课上讲解only to,用的例句是那英的"你伤害了我,还一笑而过",译成You brought pain into my life, only to have it laughed off。处于逆反期的学生,看到"小明赶火车"的例句,少不得还会幸灾乐祸,全然不会"惋惜遗憾意外"。而那英凄恻的一笑而过,拨动了少年强说愁的心弦,这个语法便自然深入人心。

"不过是一次邂逅,红楼那一场梦"里,"邂逅"是最美的中文词汇之一,美到无法简化。设想简化汉字时,如果大刀阔斧一点,省略成"解后",将不堪入目。汉字的繁体简化,普及了教育,同时也降低了标准,削弱了国人的文字领悟能力。我的英文水准停滞不前,很容易便找到了替罪羊,就是国文严重退化。

chance,是我最喜欢的英文词。如果用中文"机会"对应,显然抹杀了意境。很少有英文词能够散发出禅意,而chance透出的"因缘际会"含义,影影绰绰,挥洒不去。莘莘学子们背英文单词,动辄几万。其实,若能识得一个单词,chance,领略其朦胧与宿命,也不枉学英语一场。

誰動了我de琴弦

WHO PLUCKED MY STRINGS

小柯（词）

谁动了我的琴弦唤我到窗前
By whose hands were my strings being touched?
Coming to the window, I stood and watched.

流水浮舟你在深夜的那一边
A light boat floats as water flows;
In the other side of the night my love roams.

谁倚着我的琴枕梦尽夜满月
Who leans her head against the violin,
Dreaming a moon–lit night's dream?

还以为各自两边只能做蝴蝶
We would stay but far apart,
Each a butterfly, playing its lonely part.

谁让你我静似月
Who turned us into the moon, chill and still,

只能在心里默念
Speaking of a silent longing with a will?

檐下燕替我飞到你身边
From my roof a swallow took flight;
In my stead she would stay by your side.

谁让你我静似月
Who froze us chill and still, like the moon,

各自孤单错弄弦
Both striking wrong notes in a lonely mood?

沉夜的遥影四处风吹面
On my face the wind scattered
As the shadow of night heavily loomed.

誰動了我de琴弦

『关于蝴蝶』

狄更斯有一句话,"There are strings in the human heart that had better not be vibrated"。如此柔情,从他嘴里迸出来,殊为少见。大意是:请不要触动人的心弦。这句话,在周笔畅的声线里,却柔婉地言中了。

我喜欢歌词里的这一句:

还以为各自两边只能做蝴蝶
We would stay but far apart,
　Each a butterfly, playing its lonely part.

『关于蝴蝶』

　　中国人的蝴蝶情结，浓得化不开。记得小说《色戒》的英文版里，"生是你的人，死是你的鬼""Alive, my body belonged to you; dead, I am your ghost." Lovell 女士译得简洁传神，令人印象深刻。我想，用中国韵味的英文来翻译，可以把"ghost"改成"butterfly"。"生是你的人，死是你的蝴蝶。"老外看了，仅知文字优美，却体味不到其间氤氲的悲凉。懂英文的中国人，却心有戚戚。罗愁绮恨，痴嗔含怨，一览无遗。

　　中国人的蝴蝶情结，在梁祝里余音袅袅，西人从何领略？我曾戏言，中国人大多不信基督，许是《圣经》中某些故事与国人情结相悖。耶稣受难后三日复活，无从打动中国人心灵。倘若改为，耶稣受难后三日化蝶了呢？

　　福音里说，耶稣受难三天后，突然天地摇撼，日月无光，神的天使下凡，衣袂似雪，貌如闪电，众人悚栗惊惧。读来令人心生敬畏。而中国人更倾向看到祝英台扑向梁山伯的孤坟，大地应声而开，接纳英台入怀，蝴蝶翩跹。

　　西方悲剧里，往往英雄气短，有心杀贼，无力回天，人永远颠扑不出命运的股掌，因而产生敬畏和崇高，所以西人不似中国人向来无法无天。中国的悲剧，无论多少愁天恨海，都化成圆满的结局，把付诸行动的勇气，消解在善良的空想"阿Qism"中。

　　悲剧因凄美而渺茫，便重复上演。成千上万青年男女，重蹈前辙，焚身化蝶，葬送爱情，却听任压制人性的制度绵延千年，至今不绝。耶稣如果化蝶，中国人会长抒一口气，掌声雷动后便散了。于是千千万万的国人，前仆后继，钉上十字架，万劫不复。

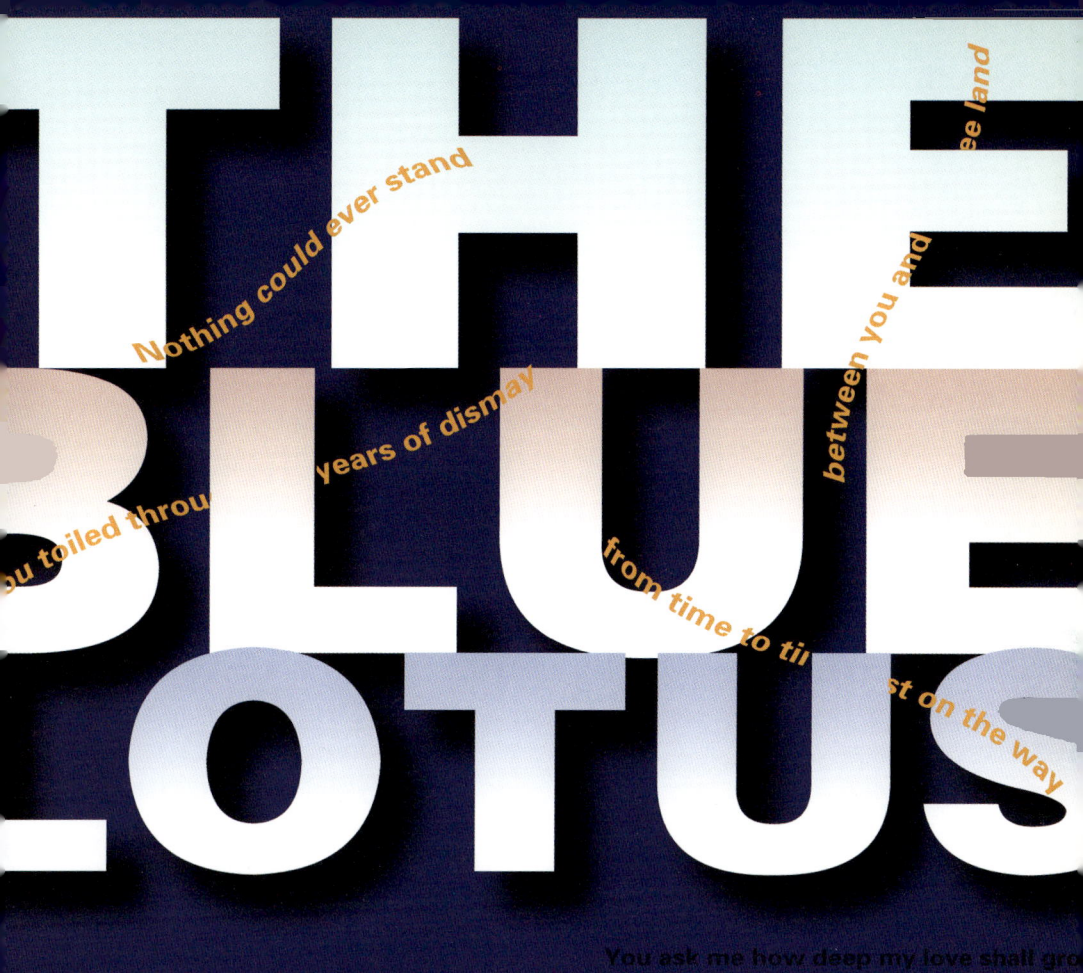

THE BLUE LOTUS

Nothing could ever stand between you and ee land
ou toiled throu years of dismay
from time to ti st on the way

A time I stumbled on the road
A time my wings broke
...no more stray
...to accept no embrace...
...ning the lotus full bloom,
...in the sky was not clear,
...ing through a wilderness
... force to break all the limits

You ask me how deep my love shall gro...
And how much I care for yo...
All my care is re...
All my love is blin...
The moon speaks of my min...
You ask me how deep my love shall gro...
And how much I care for yo...
My heart shall never chang...
By you I shall always sta...

THE MOON SPEAKS OF MY HEART
LIFE IN BURSTING BLOOM

花莲
The blue lotus

许巍（词）

没有什么能够阻挡
Nothing could ever stand

你对自由的向往
Between you and the free land.

天马行空的生涯
In a life of laissez-aller

你的心了无牵挂
All worries were blown away.

穿过幽暗的岁月
You toiled through the years of dismay,

也曾感到彷徨
From time to time lost on the way

当你低头的瞬间
Until you glanced down at your feet

才发觉脚下的路
Where your dreams and the road met.

心中那自由的世界
In the ever free wonderland,

如此的清澈高远
Clear and sublime,

盛开着永不凋零
蓝莲花
Blooms the blue lotus,
Always on its prime.

The Blue lotus

『自由』

这首歌听来格外亲切。新东方企业宣传片,以《蓝莲花》为题头曲,高亢激昂,振人心目。这首歌,让我想起校园民谣,歌中有我熟悉的菁菁校园。

十多年前我们读大学时,老狼《睡在上铺的兄弟》带来的伤感与惆怅,无以言说。记得临近毕业,总在哼一首叫做《青春》的歌:"轻轻的风轻轻的梦轻轻的晨晨昏昏,淡淡的云淡淡的泪淡淡的年年岁岁……"当年初夏校园里的苍翠气息,和着迷蒙的离愁别绪,在脑海经久不散。

20世纪90年代初,大学校园里迷茫而颓废。我们错过了60后们进大学遭遇的启蒙与激进。89年以后,大学气氛较为紧张;同时,小平南方视察,经济大潮波及校园。政治上的保守和经济上的开放并存,我们手足无措。

1993年圣诞节,似乎还有规定不得组织庆祝晚会,因为恰逢毛主席诞辰100周年。又记得1992年,全国考研报考人数只有十几万,甚至低于招生人数。88级的师兄师姐们,有的放弃了保研,在我们艳羡的注目礼中,意气风发,南下深圳海南,仿佛那里遍地金银。

相比我的大学年代,80后们的歌曲更为自信、积极与进取。《蓝莲花》的歌词,与新东方的精神别无二致,难怪如此投合。每次新东方大型活动前,我听着这首歌,总有久违的热血在激荡。

翻译这首歌里的"天马行空的生涯",我根据上下文,用了"a life of laissez-aller",一是为了与下面的"blown away"押韵,二是喜欢这个法语词,带着法兰西浪漫慵懒的气息,相当于"let do, let go"的意味。

"laissez",总是和自由、自由主义等词汇联系在一起。我崇尚自由主义。在我们的正统教育里,自由主义是一个贬义词。后来,凭借自己的阅读与体验,我才明白这不过是一个中性词,对于崇尚者来说,甚至带褒义。就像马克思主义,本身是中性词,在中国却是绝对的褒义。

在法制不健全的社会里,自由主义当然会导致放任与恣肆,肯定不受提倡。同时,又因为人们缺乏大的自由,便会在小的方面频频逾矩。我经常见到,只要没有电子眼,不少司机便扬长而去;明明竖着"禁止践踏草坪",也总有人置若罔闻;白纸黑字规定关闭小煤窑,却总有州官放火。

禁锢久了,自然得寻个渠道舒展,以资发泄。所以在强调"大一统"的中国文化里,国人却不合逻辑地如一盘散沙。这种"自由主义",少不得也是中国特色了。

Nothing between you and the free land
In a life of laissez—aller
all worries were blown away.
You toiled through the years of decay
from time to time lost on the way
until you glanced down at your feet
where your dreams and the tend air
In the ever free wonderland,
Clear and sublime,
Blooms the blue lotus,
always on its prime.

怒放的生命
LIFE IN BURSTING BLOOM

汪峰（词）

曾经多少次跌倒在路上
Many a time I stumbled on the road.

曾经多少次我折断过翅膀
Many a time my wings broke.

如今我已不再感到彷徨
Now I am no more at a loss

我想超越这平凡的生活
and mean to accept no mediocre life.

我想要怒放的生命
I am turning life into a full bloom,

就像飞翔在辽阔天空
Soaring in the sky vast and blue,

就像穿行在无边的旷野
As if trudging through a wilderness

拥有挣脱一切的力量
With a force to break all the limits.

曾经多少次失去了方向
Many a time I saw my bearings lost.

曾经多少次破灭了梦想
Many a time my dreams collapsed.

如今我已不再感到迷茫
Now I am no more aimless,

我要我的生命得到解放
Wishing to set my life free.

我想要怒放的生命
I am turning life into a full bloom,

就像矗立在彩虹之巅
Standing firm at the top of the rainbow,

就像穿行在璀璨的星河
As if wading along the river of gleaming stars

拥有超越平凡的力量
and bursting free from the commonplace.

『怒放与超越』

《怒放的生命》，激荡着青春与激情。从新东方的宣传片中，我初次听到这首歌。和《蓝莲花》一样，让人豪气盈天。2009财年的表彰大会，老俞号召我们齐唱《怒放的生命》作为闭幕曲。音乐动人心魄，我们在台上唱得荡气回肠。徐小平老师站我前排，神情投入，摇晃不止，几于癫狂。我深受鼓舞，不由得提高嗓门，声嘶力竭，直至咽炎发作，躲在人后，咳得一塌糊涂。

"怒放的生命"，在英文里，有现成的对应，即 a full bloom。可我觉得"怒放"的激昂尚未体现。用 bursting bloom，似乎贴近原意，所以标题译成 "life in busting bloom"。

歌里还有一个主题：超越平凡的生活，可以译为"go beyond the mediocre"或"accept no mediocre life"。《22条军规》的作者，美国作家 Joseph Heller 说过一句关于平庸的话，颇有意味："Some men are born mediocre men; some men achieve mediocrity; and some men had mediocrity thrust upon them."

当然，这不是 Joseph Heller 的原创，他妙笔生花，化解了莎士比亚的一句话，关于"伟大"，出自 *Twelfth Night*："Some men are born great men; some men achieve greatness; and some men had greatness thrust upon them." 大意是，有的人生来富贵，有的人是挣来的富贵，有的人是送上门的富贵。

如果把"富贵"改成"平庸",Joseph Heller的那句话,只能读者自己体味了。我近来读《22条军规》,领略其辛辣刻薄,兴味盎然,里面文学技法让我眼花缭乱,倒叙、意识流什么的,在我目前浮躁奔忙的生活状态下,无从清心尽享,便中途搁置了。

怒放生命,超越平凡。在庸庸碌碌的人群里,遗世独立,傲然绽放。在我所学的英国文学里,也有一句,一反如常的雅致,跳跃着激情。这是Tomas Moore的夏日玫瑰,百花开尽,我自怒放。

'Tis last rose of summer left blooming alone;
All her lovely companions are faded and gone.

每一次
都在徘徊孤单中坚强
In each moment of lonely hesitation
I grew even stronger;

每一次
就算很受伤
也不闪泪光
Each time I chock back tears
No matter how much it hurt,

我知道
我一直有双隐形的翅膀
I knew all along
That I had a pair of invisible wings.

带我飞
飞过绝望
To lift me up,
Leaving despair behind.

不去想
他们拥有美丽的太阳
I won't envy
Those who always enjoy the sunshine,

我看见
每天的夕阳
也会有变化
For I can enjoy as well
The beauty of change in light and shade
As the sun sets each and every day.

我知道
我一直有双隐形的翅膀
I know all along
That I have a pair of invisible wings

带我飞
给我希望
To lift me up high
In a hopeful flight.

我终于
看到
所有梦想都开花
Till at long last
I see all my dreams come into flower

追逐的年轻
歌声多嘹亮
In pursuit of a youthful song
Loud and clear.

我终于
翱翔
用心凝望不害怕
At long last
I can ride on the wind
And look into the distance
With a resolute heart,

哪里会有风
就飞多远吧
Flying as far away
As the wind can take.

隐形的翅膀
让梦恒久比天长
With the invisible wings
I will dream on and on till the end of time,

留一个
愿望
让自己想象
Leaving a wishful
Picture on my mind.

『翅膀』

隐形的翅膀,清亮悠扬。歌词似一曲奋斗的童话,听来像新东方精神的青春少女版。"追求翅膀,挑战孤单,从绝望中寻找希望,人生终将翱翔。"

有一段时期,老俞在讲座中即兴唱上几句《隐形的翅膀》,惊艳全场。后来,听说北大校长许智宏也有过演绎。英雄所见略同。老俞属老江湖,有此壮举,不足为奇。许校长身处森严体制,位高声隆,如此亲近学生,实属不易。

有一次在南昌,讲座后,当地一位大学副校长盛情相邀老俞宵夜。主方肃然围坐,比较矜持,说着没油没盐的客套。后来发现新东方人没大没小,口无遮拦,惬意率性,深受感染。在老俞一首声嘶力竭的《天路》以后,我们起哄,矛头转向这位副校长。

校长面露窘态,连连摆手拒绝,在我们几于放弃之时,竟站起身,在人群中唱了一曲水木年华的《一生有你》,摇头摆尾,双目紧闭,神色凄绝,载歌载舞。我们当时戏称要录下来,放在大学网上供学生观赏,该校长人气一定大增。看来,不少高校校长不得不端着架子,示其威仪,其实都不乏真性情。

大家喜欢《隐形的翅膀》,不知是否源于歌词里的灰姑娘,柔弱却坚忍,目光里永远闪烁着期冀与渴望。那么,隐形的翅膀,应该是指灰姑娘心中的信念。可惜翻译时,选择了直译:wings invisible。我曾经想用 veiled wings,或者 wings unseen。形容词颠来倒去,也无从割舍,干脆直译了。

希腊神话里,伊卡瑞斯(Icarus)插上翅膀,逃离绝望,越飞越高,不顾翅膀上的蜡逐渐融化,坠入大海。虽具悲剧色彩,但对希望、梦想和翱翔的渴望,却和《隐形的翅膀》异曲同工。伊卡瑞斯也曾给予了余光中同样的灵感:

你是挣不脱的夸父
飞不起来的伊卡瑞斯
每天一次的轮回
从曙到暮
扭不屈之颈,昂不垂之头

会呼吸的痛

PAIN THAT CAN BREATHE

姚若龙（词）

没看你脸上张扬过哀伤
I never see sadness dance on your face

那是种多么寂寞的倔强
With a stubborn loneliness.

你拆了城墙让我去流浪
Tearing down the wall of protection,
You reduce me into a vagabond,

在原地等我把自己捆绑
And stay where you were,
Yet leaving me to bind myself down.

你没说你也会软弱
You never speak of your weak moments

需要依赖我
When you need me to be there.

我就装不晓得
So I might as well pretend ignorance

自由移动自我地过
And live a life as free as the air.

想念是会呼吸的痛
Yearning is a pain that can breathe,

它活在我身上所有角落
Filling up every corner of me.

哼你爱的歌会痛
It hurts when humming a favorite tune of yours,

看你的信会痛连沉默也痛
And when reading your letters as silence falls.

遗憾是会呼吸的痛
Regrets are a pain that can breathe,

它流在血液中来回滚动
Rushing in my blood, and never freeze.

后悔不贴心会痛
It hurts when regretting being always blind,

恨不懂你会痛
When failing to read your mind,

想见不能见最痛
And when ever missing each other,
Yet can never be together.

『英语名词化趋势』

"没看你脸上张扬过哀伤"？提笔翻译，这句话颇费踌躇。语境是"……多么寂寞的倔强"，体现出隐忍与坚强。平直一点，可以用"your face was never written with sadness"，但"张扬"和坚韧无从表达。灵光一现，我尝试用"sadness dance on your face"。这个dance举重若轻，轻灵中反衬无奈和沉郁。

不过，相比中文，在书面语中，英语更倾向于用名词。比如"你没说你也会软弱"，这里的动词或形容词"软弱"，不如改为名词词组weak moments，这样，you never speak of your weak moments符合英文习惯，也更雅致。

同样，"我就装不晓得"里的"不晓得"，是动词，英文一般会用名词ignorance，就像"没来"，会用absence，"我不抽烟"，用"I am no smoker"一样。阿杜曾唱道，"我闭上眼睛就是天黑"。"闭上眼睛"如果用close的动词形式when I close my eyes，一定没有名词形式简洁传神：a close of eyes brings night into my life。

不过，中文里词性活用更为普遍。这种思维大量进入洋泾浜英语。经典例子是long time no see，把see用成名词，极富创意，以至于被英美人吸纳进了英文。洋泾浜里还有一句更为精练，"不能"就是"no can"。英国文豪萧伯纳居然也被折服，曾说过，no can比正规英文里的"unable"更为生动鲜活，朗朗上口。

现今，但凡和中国文化沾点边的，都风靡欧美，洋泾浜英语自不例外。前两年英国有部畅销书，*A Chinese-English Dictionary for Lovers*，出自旅英华人作家Guo Xiaolu，通篇中式英文语法，比如"I not met you yet, you in future"，等等，助动词全被省略，反而言简意赅。字里行间带着诡谲的异国情调，怎不令老外沉迷？

认真的雪

SNOW WITH ALL MY HEART

薛之谦（词）

夜深人静 那是爱情
Deep and quiet at night

偷偷地控制着我的心
Love steals in and seizes my heart,

提醒我 爱你要随时待命
Telling me to keep standing by.

音乐安静 还是爱情啊
Silence sets in as music dies

一步一步吞噬着我的心
When love again gnaws my heart.

爱上你我失去了我自己
In the drama of love I've lost my part.

认真的雪
SNOW WITH ALL MY HEART

爱得那么深 爱得那么认真
I was deep in love with all my heart,

可还是听见了你说不可能
Only to see you depart.

已经十几年没下雪的上海突然飘雪
Snow broke out in Shanghai,
An absence of more than ten years,

就在你说了分手的瞬间
The moment you told me to break up.

雪下得那么深 下得那么认真
The snow lies thick, falling with all my heart,

倒映出我躺在雪中的伤痕
And revealing my snowy bruises of love.

我并不在乎自己究竟多伤痕累累
How much it hurts means little to me,

可我在乎今后你有谁陪
But could you ever find a better company to keep?

"认真的雪"在英文里,直译应该是snow in earnest,若想加重语气,用snow in real earnest。我觉得未达歌中况味。雪沉沉地下,人痴痴地恋。用心良苦,付诸雪花,寄托怀抱。翻成snow with all my heart,会不会好一点呢?

　　With one's heart表示心无旁骛,尽心尽意。如果雪兀自努力飘落,应该是 it snows with all it's heart。而雪本无心,人自有意,所以我用snow with all my heart。是否指代错误?估计难逃语法的清规戒律。就像在《发如雪》里,"我锁眉……"我译成"Hard and sad I knit my brows…"这里,sad明显应该为sadly,才符合语法。但在语法正确和韵律两者间,我自然选择后者。

　　歌曲前几句里,夜深人静,音乐迷离,心碎无痕。英国诗人罗塞蒂的妹妹Christina Rossetti有一首诗,似同出一辙:

Lie still, lie still, my breaking heart
My silent heart, lie still and break.
平静,平静,我破碎的心呵
我悄无声息的心呵,静静破碎。

　　Christina Rossetti的诗,当年颇受徐志摩、吴宓等大家的青睐。徐志摩翻译过她的一首song。据我考据,徐志摩把其中两句,"And if thou wilt, remember, And if thou wilt, forget."化解在自己最美的诗《偶然》里:

"你我相逢在黑夜的海上,
　你有你的,我有我的,方向;
　你记得也好,
　最好你忘掉
　在这交会时互放的光亮!"

回到《认真的雪》。这首歌浅显直白,唯"吞噬"一词值得探讨。"吞噬我的心",我没有用"吞"的"swallow",而用 it gnaws my heart。gnaw,咬噬,这个词和"心"连接,英文里更为妥帖。

《圣经·约伯记》里有一句,"And the pains that gnaw me take no rest."(Job 30:17)疼痛啃噬,无休无止。圣经里的英文,美不胜收。一些章节,字字珠玑。传道书和约伯记,有宿命苍凉哀伤笼罩其间,曾让我手不释卷,欲罢不能。一个gnaw字,让约伯悲切的眼神在我眼前闪烁。身上疼痛,心中悲哀,那个约伯依然虔敬笃信,卑微善良。

DEATH WON'T DO US PART
THE PASSENGER
A RECORDED MEMORY

生死不离，你的梦落在哪里
Where did your dreams fall, I wonder.
We shall never part, whether in this world or another.

想着生活继续
And life shall carry on.

天空失去美丽，你却等待明天站起
Even the beauty of the sky dies
you keep waiting for tomorrow to rise.

无论你在哪里，我都要找到你
Wherever you are, I am coming to you.

血脉能创造奇迹
The same blood rushing in us can work miracles

你的呼喊就刻在我的血液里
for in my blood your cry forever echoes.

生死不离，我数秒等你消息
No death shall do us part;
I counted the seconds to hear from you.

相信生命不息
That life goes on is all I knew.

我看不到你，你却牵挂在我心里
You are nowhere to be seen,
Yet always on my mind as have been.

无论你在哪里，我都要找到你
Wherever you are, I am coming to you.

血脉能创造奇迹
The same blood rushing in us can work miracles.

搭起双手筑成你回家的路基
Hand in hand we are laying your homeward roads.

生死不离，全世界都被沉寂
No death shall do us part,
Even in dead silence the whole world fell apart.

痛苦也不哭泣
Shed no tears in bitter pain,

爱是你的传奇，彩虹在风雨后升起
The legend of love lifts a rainbow
After the wind and rain.

无论你在哪里，我都要找到你
Wherever you are, I am coming to you.

血脉能创造奇迹
The same blood rushing in us can work wonders;

你一丝希望是我全部的动力
I am holding on for life as your hope flickers.

『 汶川 』

  2008年春夏之交,无论何时何地，总能听到这首歌在电台、电视台回响。还有一首，更为痛切，叫《我知道你会来》，每每听到"你什么时候来……我正拼命赶来，我会坚持到我看到你……"便难以自持。不忍想象，那些生命，鲜活的，跳跃的，那些希望，坚强的，执着的，怎么会一丝一缕，从这个世界消散了呢？

  Angela Topping是当代英国女诗人，50多岁，职业是英语教师。她有一首关于地震的诗录入诗集Can You Hear《你可曾听见？》，模拟一名压在废墟下孩子的语气，读了令人百感丛生。回顾汶川地震，更添唏嘘。我不擅英汉翻译，草草译就如下：

Whether to cry out in answer to
my father's straggled cries.
As he shifts bricks above my head.
Or whether to keep silent, holding back
This dust with damped lips. I lie
Sealed in and can not choose.

爸爸
你在搬我头顶的砖
我是应该哭喊
回应你遥远沉闷的呼唤
还是紧咬牙关
挡住呛人的尘土
我
躺在尘封的世界里
无从选择

If I speak, death will steal my breath
Seeping in at my mouth;
If I choose silence he may go away
And weep, and never know how close
My grave was, how I longed to answer.

如果开口
死神充塞我嘴
夺走呼吸
如果选择沉默
爸爸将废然离去
痛哭失声
永不知晓
我的坟墓
近在咫尺
也永不知晓
我曾多么渴望
回应他的呼唤

  我不忍想象，汶川地震废墟下的孩子们，是如何满嘴满眼满鼻尘土，身上万钧重负，剧痛阵阵袭来，头上的凄厉呼唤似隐似现，心里的渴望一丝丝升腾，又一缕缕断绝。

  汶川，you bled my blood, let me cry your tears。

64

笔记
A Recorded Memory

黄友桢（词）

我看见天空很蓝
Blue and clear is the sky,

就像你在我身边的温暖
As warm as when you were by my side.

生命有太多遗憾
More to come, yet more to miss,

人越成长越觉得孤单
As one grows up to even bitter loneliness.

我很想飞多远都不会累
I long to fly, and shall never weary,

才明白爱得越深心就会越痛
Only to see I loved deep, yet hurt deep.

我只想飞在我的天空飞
I wish to fly in my own sky,

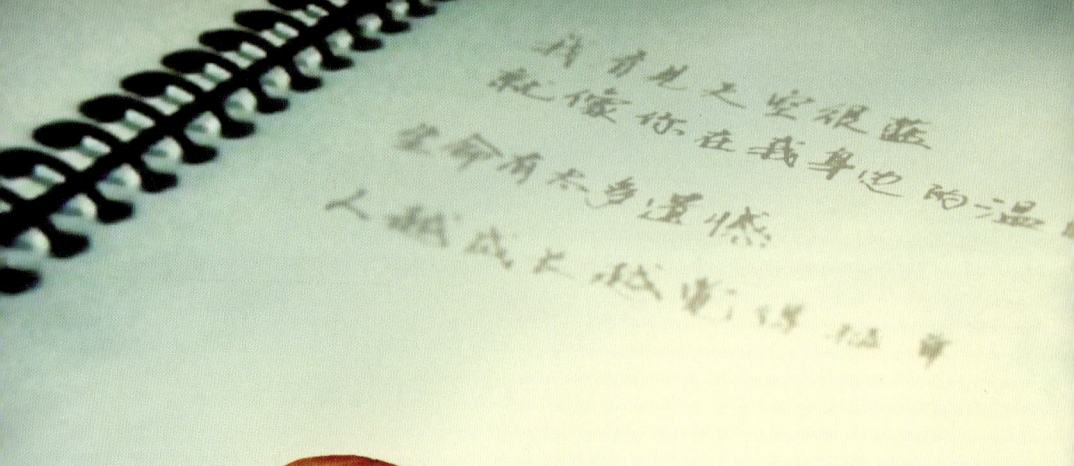

我知道你会在我身边
Knowing you'll be there by my side.

回忆的画面记录的语言
There are images and words in a recorded memory

爱始终是你手中长长的线
Where love was a long thread between you and me.

载着我的想念飞过了地平线
Flying beyond the horizon, carrying my longing

你温暖的笑脸还一如从前
Till your smile comes back, ever heart-warming.

回忆的画面记录的语言
There are images and words in a recorded memory

你说要我学着勇敢一点
Where you told me to keep up my courage,

偶尔哭红双眼你一定会了解
Knowing that I cried my eyes red now and then

眼泪是我心中另一种完美
For my tears are no less of a happy end.

『关于周笔畅』

《笔记》的曲调，满怀憧憬，又带一丝青涩，恍然与伤感，与《隐形的翅膀》同属成长题材歌曲，也符合周笔畅清亮的声线。不知为何取名《笔记》。指日记中记载的回忆？不得而知。我自作主张，翻译为a recorded memory，取意"一段记载的回忆"。

维基百科里，对周笔畅有着详细的介绍，我读了暗暗称奇。"洋鬼子"对中国了如指掌，把中文网页里都搜不到的信息，比如她父母的名字，以及一些童年生活细节，全部一一列举。关于《笔记》，维科翻译的是 Bibi's Notes，也挺有创意。

Bibi这个英文名比较少见。前段时间，美籍华裔作家谭恩美的最新小说 *Saving Fish from Drowning* 里，主人公是一位华裔老太太，也叫Bibi。Bibi作为英文名，有Bebe和Beebee两种变体，都可以追溯到波斯的名字。周笔畅取这个英文名，倒是和她的中文拼音珠联璧合。

引用几句维基百科里的英文，在了解周笔畅的同时，还能学学英文：

Zhou has been brought up in a family where music permeates everyday life. Her mother, being a music teacher and singer herself, is an avid fan of Chinese folk music. When Zhou was a child, her grandmother taught her to play the piano.

这里我们了解到,周笔畅的家庭,洋溢着音乐的氛围,"where music permeates everyday life"。

她的妈妈是一名音乐老师,热爱民乐,"an avid fan of Chinese folk music"。周笔畅儿时,在外婆的指导下学习钢琴。

百科的简介里,还谈到2005年,周笔畅在广州初次参加超女试听的一个细节:

The then 19-year-old showed up the day of the audition in her father's old oversize jacket without a trace of makeup. In her own words, she just rolled out of bed before going to the audition and did not even get a chance to wash her face. Her boyish attire almost made the security guard stop her at the entrance because the contest was supposed to be for girls only.

说19岁的笔笔穿着爸爸宽大的夹克,素面朝天,仿佛翻身下床,连脸都来不及洗就来了(she just rolled out of bed before going to the audition and did not even get a chance to wash her face)。守门人甚至将她拦在门外,声称超女比赛只准女生参加。

作为百科全书,叙述这样生动的细节,倒是别有生趣。

乘客
THE PASSENGER

林夕（词）

高架桥过去了
The overpass has been passed;

路口还有好多个
Many crossings are yet to come.

这旅途不曲折
Not much twists and turns along the way,

一转眼就到了
In a blink of an eye it's over.

坐你开的车
A ride along in your car,
……

高架桥过去了
The overpass has been passed;

路口还有好多个
Many crossings are yet to come.

这旅途不曲折
Not much twists and turns along the way,

一转眼就到了
In a blink of an eye it's over.

坐你开的车
A ride along in your car,

听你听的歌
To listen to your songs,

我们好快乐
What a great time!

第一盏路灯开了
The first street lamp turns on.

你在想什么
What's on your mind

歌声好快乐
Amidst the joyful music?

坐你开的车
A ride along in your car

听你听的歌
Listening to your songs

我不是不快乐
I am not unhappy.

白云苍白色
But pale is the white cloud;

蓝天灰蓝色
And gray is the blue sky.

我家快到了
And my home is around the corner.

我是这部车
I am the first

第一个乘客
Passenger in your car.

我不是不快乐
I am not unhappy.

天空血红色
But ruddy is the sky at dusk;

『王菲的歌』

　　王菲经典歌曲无以计数，我却偏爱《乘客》。我研究文学，以淡淡的忧伤为最高境界，声嘶力竭的爱与生死，不属于至高至美的文学。《乘客》婉转低回，哀而不伤，是我喜爱的理由。这首歌的意境，我觉得适合一篇短篇小说，比如现代版的《边城》，以悬而未决的哀愁，无疾而终。

　　《乘客》的粤语版取名《花事了》，弥漫着佛教的宿命。《红楼梦》里麝月抽取花名签，得到荼蘼花。宋代王淇有一句："开到荼蘼花事了。"荼蘼在春天最后凋谢，作为一场绚烂花事的谢幕。花事已了，一切皆空，Gone is the flowering season。

　　王菲还有很多歌值得翻译，列举如下：

　　我上大学时，《容易受伤的女人》炙手可热，翻成Woman Vulnerable to Hurt，太直白生硬，可能不及Delicate Woman或Fragile Woman简洁。

《执迷不悔》,No Regrets Ever 或者Remorseless Woman。《爱与痛的边缘》,The Brink of Love and Pain。《但愿人长久》,Wish We shall Last Forever。《暗涌》,Undercurrents。《将爱》,About to Love。

《棋子》,A Helpless Chess Piece。没有比一枚棋子更helpless的事了。

《我愿意》,应该是取自婚礼誓言的回答,用Yes, I Do比较适合。但在这首歌的语境下,就得用I Am Most Willing了。

《红豆》,Read Beans。许渊冲老先生在翻译王维的《红豆》时,译成love seeds,十分传神。记得最后一句,"此物最相思",译为they would revive fond memories。

《流年》,The Flow of Time。译成英文,也有挥散不去的苍凉。

一千年以后
IN A THOUSAND YEARS

李瑞洵（词）

心跳乱了节奏
My heart has lost its rhythm,

梦也不自由
My dreams no longer carefree.

爱时的绝对承诺不说
The promise withheld when still in love

沉到一千年以后
Has sunk into an abyss a thousand years later.

放任无奈淹没尘埃
Dust gives way to floods of regrets

我在废墟之中守着你走来
When I keep watch for you in ruins.

我的泪光承载不了
My glistening tears can't bear the weight

所有一切你要的爱
Of all the love you thirst for.

因为在一千年以后
In a thousand years

世界早已没有我
The world will have lost me,

无法深情挽着你的手
No way to hold your hand in fondness,

浅吻着你额头
And dip a light kiss on your forehead.

别等到一千年以后
Don't wait till a thousand years later

所有人都遗忘了我
When I shall pass into oblivion.

那时红色黄昏的沙漠
Then over a red desert at dusk,

能有谁
Is there anyone

解开刹那千年的寂寞
Who would ever undo a loneliness

刹那千年的寂寞
Over a time spanning a thousand years?

『时间』

公元1009年。我是一个仪态从容，身形瘦削的才子，在晓风残月中迷醉。而梦里，塞外黑云催逼，羌笛悠悠，叹此身不是龙城飞将，怎堪山河残破，空悲切！

公元2009年。我是一个面容模糊的博友，隐身于成千上万个同类中，把思想敲给冰冷的键盘，变成光怪陆离的文字，在屏幕上隐隐约约地闪烁，语焉不详。

公元1009年。秦淮河边，树影婆娑。我的视线越过如云的红裙，跌落在塞北的呼啸朔风里，映着金戈铁马的惨白寒光。却有纤纤玉手，擎起盈盈酒杯，在耳边说："可惜明年花更好，知与谁同？"

公元2009年。我坐在电脑面前，翻译林俊杰的《一千年以后》，歌声里，风雨飘摇中的北宋才子，裹挟着奢靡浮华，款款走来，仿佛一场千年尘梦。

沧桑，苍凉，苍茫，是中国的时间概念，动辄就是千年的誓言与等待。个中滋味，不足为外人道。记得有一年在重庆，老俞和我们去看大足石刻。满山石刻气势恢弘，依山而建，与山脉浑然一体，仰之弥高。

我所关心的，是当年的那些石匠。他们历时250多年，筚路蓝缕，留下珍贵遗产。我问老俞，"现代科技发达，倾其全力，需多久能再造一山石雕"。老俞的回答，大意是现代人非无能，只是无心而为。这种事功，有赖精神力量的支撑。而且，"古代人没有时间概念，"老俞说，"这样才能创造奇迹"。

现代人习惯了一句话，时间就是金钱。可是，那里一千多年前，人头攒动，汗洒如雨，时间的痕迹只是晨钟暮鼓，春花秋月，是人们脸上掩映着的斑驳树影。工匠里，一定会有一个叫富贵或有财的汉子。每日闻鸡而作，粗糙的大手紧紧攥着榔头和凿子，一下，又一下，火星四溅，直至日落西山。

　　漫山遍野，叶子黄了，又重归青翠。花儿落了，复又飞上枝头。有霜白悄然爬上富贵或有财的鬓角，直至华发满头。富贵或有财的儿孙，从他颤巍巍的手里，接过愈久弥坚的凿子，日出而作，日落而息。岁月悠悠而逝，瑰丽堂皇的石刻终于扑入人们眼帘。富贵或有财坟头蔓延的菁菁青草，早已耸立成参天大树。在一千多年后，有山风掠过，依然婆娑作响。

　　老俞说得对，中国古人没有时间概念，大时无形，因而现代意义的效率和效益，在他们面前苍白无力。古人对未来的认识模糊而遥远，他们活在当下的专注里。现代人争得了时间，赚足了金钱，攥住了幸福，得到了享乐。富贵或有财听任似水流年，渐行渐远。他们用时间，换来的不是pleasure,也不是happiness,而是（何兆武先生语）blessedness.

　　我艳羡不已。千年的寂寞，废墟与承诺，能换来Blessedness，天福，上天赐予的至福。

几句武侠英译

我喜欢把中国特色的事物译成英文，乐此不疲。武侠英文，挑战不小。有些词几乎无法翻译，比如穴位，我不知中医英文是怎么翻的，pivotal joints, or paralytic points？"九阴白骨爪"等武术招式，更是无从下笔。"The palm of ghastly bones in the ninth Yin"？

权当练笔，我举几个武侠英译的例子：
他心中一寒："此人轻功，果然在我之上。"

"He certainly beats me," he shuddered. "He is much better at Lightness Kungfu than I am."

嗤嗤嗤数声连响，身后忽然射出七八件暗器，分向他袭去。

There came whizzing sounds in quick succession before seven or eight secret weapons sprang from behind, aiming straight at him.

长剑出鞘，一招"流星赶月"，剑锋却已指向对方胸口。

No soon had he whipped out the sword to practice the Meteor Chasing the Moon than the keen blade was already pointed to the chest of his opponent.

手腕一沉，避开了这一剑。

He sank his wrist to ward off the impending blow.

她两只手轻轻一拂，指缝间突然飞出十余道银光。接着，就是一连串的惨呼。

With a whisk of her hands, a dozen or so silvery rays of lights flashing out between her fingers, only to be followed by screams in agony here and there.

她闭上眼睛，叹息着道："好好的一双手不用来绣花，却用来杀人，真是可惜得很……"

"What a pair of hands…" she sighed, closing her eyes, " pity that they are not meant for embroidery, but for killing."

一个剑客的光芒与生命，往往就在他手里握着的剑上。

The glory and life of a swordsman lie in the very sword clenched in his hands.

但剑若也有情，它的光芒是否也就会变得和流星一样短促。

Yet given a feeling of its own, the sword would soon burn its glow out, fleeting as a meteor.

一段武汉话英译

在口译方面，我只有客串的资格，离专业水准相去甚远。2001年我还在武大英文系，一位老教授退休，一时没有中年梯队接续，系里退而求其次，让我顶上了。诚惶诚恐中，我买了当时市面上所有的口译书，潜心研读，费尽心思，总算没让学生给哄下台，幸甚至哉。

我喜欢一些稀奇古怪，没有定论的翻译。中国诗词、典籍、文论、武侠，等等。有一次口译课，我另辟蹊径，举了一段武汉话的翻译实例。

去医院看病，有个小青年不排队，往队里插。

有人喊："出来出来，插个么队吵？"

小青年说："嚷么事嚷？王医生是我亲戚。"

那人说："伙计，闹个么眼子吵？又冒得那个哈数。"

这段话的精髓在这句"闹眼子"。在中国方言里，离文化中心起源越远，古文成分愈多，如粤语。武汉话属楚语，也保留了一些。比如"陈米"，表示旧米，去年的米。小青年，叫"小糙子"。武汉人对一些家禽动物，称鸡子、鸭子、狗子、羊子。不知是否取的像管子、韩非子、列子中"子"的尊称。如此看来，武汉人是最早的动物保护主义者了。

闹眼子，从书面角度讲，大意是闹个眼球，吸引注意。最直接的英文对应可以是"horse around"，表示瞎闹腾，比如小孩胡闹什么的。但用在不同的场合，得分别对待。要是你称赞某人一段当众演讲或表演精彩，那人自谦道，"哪里哪里，闹个眼子而已。"这里就不好翻。用"Nothing much, I am flattered"还是"I am only making fun of myself"？

上段话，我与之对应的英文是：

In a hospital, some people were queuing up to see a doctor, when a young man tried to cut in.
A voice yelled, "Get out! What are you doing here?"
"Do you have to yell?" the young man retorted. "Doctor Wang is a relative of mine！"
The man sneered, "What tricks are you playing, man? Who do you think you are？"

我用的词比较文雅，尽管应该加上bloody或hell之类，以符合武汉的场景以及武汉人的暴躁性格。自从两岁的时候户口迁到武汉，我在这里已经生活了三十多年，大小事基本知晓，也越来越喜欢这里的人与事。

武汉人性格豪爽，俗不可耐，却有可爱的一面。如果街上碰上车辆轻微擦碰，会立刻招来幸灾乐祸的惊呼："哟嗬，擂（撞）了！"并迅速聚拢大群兴奋的闲人。但如果真是稍微大一点的事故，武汉人会人人争先，奋不顾身，不求回报，危难中总是感人至深。

遗憾的是，我至今不会说武汉话。要是武汉人看到我翻译武汉话，少不得也会斥道："伙计，你还翻译武汉话，莫在这里闹眼子了。"也是。搁笔，洗了睡算了。

武汉话『你嚇我』的英译

武汉话"你嚇我"是一句感叹词，音"和"，即"你吓我"，表示极度诧异。举一个语境：清晨，飞驰而过的公汽上，甩出一碗吃剩的热干面。目击者错愕，"你嚇我，素质这差？准头这低？要是老子，准能甩到花坛里！"

译成英语，可以直接用语气词，譬如"Oooops"，"boy"，"oh, my"或者"gosh"之类。若是英伦窈窕淑女，少不得会轻掩朱唇，嘤的一声，"Dear me!"及时摸出香料包，凑到鼻前，双目紧闭，乘势歪在芳心暗属的绅士怀里。

在很多情况下，翻译得看语境。设想一道武汉话英译试题如下：

那天，小倩在操场掷铁饼，铁饼却擦着陈老师的头皮过去。小倩惊呼："你嚇我！"陈老师余悸未消，说，"这哪里是我嚇你吵，明明是你在嚇我。"

前面一部分翻译好说,按部就班:

The other day, Xiaoqian was throwing a discus on the sports ground . The discus, however, narrowly missed Mr. Chen. Xiaoqian cried out.

后面的"你嚇我",以小倩的淑女口吻说出来,并不需要语气词,根据上下文,可以是"That was close!",相当于"好险!"

陈老师后面的那句可就棘手了:"这哪里是我嚇你吵,明明是你在嚇我。"在此性命攸关之际,陈老师也许弃了师道尊严,唾句美式俚语,"heck!"较为符合语境。也跟"嚇"的武汉话发音接近。

"heck"是"hell"的委婉语,相当于中文里的"靠!"把"c"改为"k"的委婉语。不过,"这哪里是我嚇你吵,明明是你在嚇我"。这句武汉话博大精深,一个"heck"仅仅体现皮毛。没有武汉话英译的8级水准,断不能胜任翻译。你嚇我,只能放弃了。

我和谁都不争

在《听杨绛谈往事》里,又一次听到耄耋老人喃喃自语,"就剩我一个了",令人中心痛伤。回想起《我们仨》里的惴惴忧思,意绪难平,几于无以为继。

杨绛先生曾引用过 Walter Savage Landor 的 "I strove with none,我和谁都不争"里的两句话。Landor 的诗句,一贯精致典雅,简洁隽永。全诗如下:

I strove with none, for none was worth my strife.
Nature I loved and, next to Nature, Art:
I warm'd both hands before the fire of life;
It sinks, and I am ready to depart.

大意是:　　我和谁都不争,
　　　　　　和谁争我都不屑。
　　　　　　我先爱过大自然,
　　　　　　又爱过艺术。
　　　　　　我双手烤着,
　　　　　　生命之火取暖。
　　　　　　火萎了,
　　　　　　我也准备走了。

用这首诗来描述杨绛先生,再妥帖不过。读到这里,我看到书中98岁的先生近照,茕茕孑立,却不见悲欣,浅笑淡定,我突然心中大恸。

读大师的故事,体会自己的渺小与无知,殊为一桩幸事。说来惭愧,在读《听杨绛谈往事》之前,由于钱锺书的光芒遮蔽,我对杨绛先生的学识知之甚少。现在了解她是清华外文系研究生毕业，师从梁宗岱、吴宓、叶公超等大家，又陪同钱锺书，在牛津旁听西方文学，满腹经纶，后来小说、剧本、译著等身。

好歹我也算学英国文学出身，书中所提及的作者大多知晓。看到杨绛在牛津图书馆，"从Chaucer开始，一个一个经典作家按文学史往下读，主要作品一部一部从头到尾细读……"我背上冷汗涔涔。

读研时，我被动地看了一些书，基本浅尝辄止。老师吩咐的每星期阅读经典原作，不少都置之脑后，仅凭自己兴趣，读点情节梗概和评论以敷衍。记得老师布置读George Eliot的 *Middlemarch*，足有七八百页。班上有勤奋的女生，通读了全篇，我觉得不可思议。见杨绛说她很喜欢George Eliot，我追悔莫及。

"我和谁都不争"，是杨先生淡泊一生的写照。可在牛津，杨绛和钱锺书依然有过竞争，比赛谁读的书多。年终结算，大体相当。只是钱锺书读的都是大部头，杨绛把小册子也充了数。钱锺书还没算上中文书，何况有的书还读了几遍。

想想我们现代人，蝇营狗苟，逐名趋利，争的都是身外之物。把自我的修为与陶染，视同草芥，最终心为形役，挣扎，分裂，绝望。争小利者，必失大节。从杨绛先生"不争"的心理，我看到了博大。

一直期待有一天，能去牛津大学旁听历史和文学，不求文凭。这符合我的阅读习惯，只为阅读快感，既不愿和人探讨，也不为什么提升、充实、改造之类。那一年，在牛津小镇的金色阳光里，我恋恋忘返。当时没读这本书，不然少不得要去Norham Gardens，凭吊一下钱锺书和杨绛的足迹。

真想在小镇上闲闲地住几年，上午读西方文学，下午翻阅中文线装书，从微曦到薄暮。这一梦想，不知何时得以实现？

麦秋已过

落叶满阶,肃然秋矣。武汉总是四季分明。

突然想起《圣经》里的一句话:"麦秋已过,夏令已完,我们还未得救。"(The harvest is past, the summer has ended, and we are not saved.)我不是基督徒,《耶利米书》里,上帝的震怒和子民的哀鸣,在我脑海里没有印象。我只是喜欢这句话的苍凉和宿命。

我能想象的,是农人在高高谷堆前,阵阵凉风中,张惶四顾,怅然若失。农忙的热火朝天,依稀还在耳际,眼前的麦田却早已疏疏落落。农人瑟瑟蹲下来,收紧敞开的衣襟,布满老茧的双手搓着几枚麦粒,若有所思。

2008年奥运盛况空前,已成为过去。股市楼市却依然低迷。奥运并没有成为一次明显的分水岭。人们从2001年开始的翘首以盼,没有等到柳暗花明。目前应着眼的,还是本分的生活和踏实的迈步。

回想起小时候春游,盼得寝食不安,最终意尽而返,书包里剩下油腻腻的蛋糕渣,挤瘪的煮鸡蛋,头上插着残花败柳,深一脚浅一脚,余兴未消。想到即将到来的期中考试,不由得垂头丧气,心头阴霾密布。

英国诗人布莱克写过一部《地狱箴言》*Proverbs of the Hell*,开篇第一句是"In seed time learn, in harvest teach, in winter enjoy."春天求学,秋季教诲,冬日享受。什么意思?我没读懂,只是喜欢Blake的简约与神秘。

关于博客

我自2007年1月底滥竽博客行列。承蒙网友青睐,点击量竟攀升过百万。对新兴事物,我向来敬而远之,此番却亲历其盛。

我总在想,近两百万轻轻的"click"声后面,是什么时空?什么面容?什么心情?你们是谁?你们有什么样的声音?话语?呼吸?

> Between
> Your eye and this page
> I am standing

"我,站在你的视线和页面之间……" 这是Hafiz的一首小诗Between your eye and this page首句。Hafiz是14世纪伊朗神秘主义诗人,其诗歌幽深隽永,耐人寻味。每逢重大事件,如就业、前途、婚嫁、出行,伊朗人常用哈菲兹的诗文占卦。在1997年5月23日总统大选中,有人照此占卦,诗文中竟出现了哈塔米的名字,一语中谶,传诵一时。

哈菲兹700多年前的喃喃自语,穿越冥冥时空,预言了我现在的状态:站在你们的视线和电脑页面之间,忐忑,惶恐,感激,不知所措。我知道,这一刻,我的心情和文字,在光标的闪烁中跃上页面,几分钟之后,你的视线,便悄无声息,纷至沓来。

有一年,我参加新东方"梦想之旅",从南京、马鞍山、芜湖、安庆、九江、黄石、黄冈、武汉、荆州、宜昌一路溯江而上。每到一地,登上网络,打开页面,便有你的视线破空而来。雁过寒潭,风入疏竹。这个spaceless的space,永远机缘际会,风流云散。

中国的博客和读者群体，蔚然大观。而在发源地美国，除了播客火热，博客大多冷冷清清，门可罗雀。中国人含蓄内敛，深藏不露，便诉诸文字，寄托怀抱。同时又喜窃窃私语，窥视他人，鄙视隐私。这种传统由来已久，便反映在博客现象上。

时代周刊曾把年度风云人物桂冠给了YOU——全体网民。中国的芸芸博客，恐怕难免再次黄袍加身。我躬逢其盛，自然和你们一起，共享殊荣。这些年来，我在中英文书籍里心醉沉迷，杂览闲读，不能自拔。读书成了了无止境的过程，不图利禄功名。眼睛勤快，笔头却庸懒了。若不是博客这个任务，提笔想必遥遥无期。若不是你们的点击，早已失却信心，无以为继了。谢谢你们的鼓励和宽容。

在那首小诗里，Hafiz最后说：
    Between
    Your eye and this page
    Hafiz
    Is standing

    Bump
    Into me
    More

"我，站在你的视线和页面之间……请赐我更多的邂逅。"

一首戏谑的英文诗

诗的题目是"上帝对我说过yes"。God said yes to me。

作者是美国当代诗人Kaylin Haught。语言轻快戏噱,以一个时尚女孩的口吻质询上帝,而上帝却是一个女教师,慈祥和气,体贴开明。诗歌的大意是,It is good to be different and be whatever you are and to do whatever you want.

我的英译汉水平一向拙劣,从未示人,此番尝试如下,以期抛砖引玉。

I asked God if it was okay to be melodramatic
我问上帝,我可以多愁善感吗?

And she said yes
上帝说,可以。

I asked her if it was okay to be short
我问上帝,我个子矮,也可以吗?

And she said it sure is
她说,当然可以。

I asked her if I could wear nail polish
我问她,我能涂指甲油,

Or not wear nail polish
还是不能。

And she said honey
她说，甜心

She calls me that sometimes
（她有时这样叫我）

She said you can do just exactly

What you want to
她说，你想做什么就做什么。

Thanks God I said
谢谢你，上帝。我说。

And is it okay even if I don't paragraph

My letters
另外，我写信不分段也可以吗？

Sweet cakes God said
小甜糕，上帝说。

Who knows where she picked that up
（鬼知道她从哪里学到这个称呼）

What I'm telling you is

Yes, yes, yes
我跟你说，可以，可以，可以。

吴宓翻译的一首英文诗

近来读《吴宓日记续编》，对这位国学和英文双料大师兴趣浓厚。吴宓曾任清华国学所主任，是钱锺书的老师，与汤用彤、陈寅恪并称"哈佛三杰"。后来为保守的"学衡派"主将，维护文言文地位，被鲁迅骂个半死。又一辈子为情所困，学问上了了而终。

20本的日记，历时几十年，记载所思所为，社会变迁，情场纠葛，事无巨细，却不亚于宏篇巨制。吴宓在1947年赴武大任外文系主任，50年后，我有幸留校，不知可否尊吴宓为老领导？忽而国文系主任，转而外文系主任，又曾是史学系主任。噫嘻，怎不令人五体投地？

吴宓日记里，我看到一个细节，说他20世纪50年代和学生刘炳善谈话，奖掖后学。"外二学生刘炳善来……宓劝刘生专心学业，另求恋爱对象云云。"（1951年4月14日日记）想起大学里学的《英国文学简史》，作者就是刘炳善。后来为了考研，曾背得滚瓜烂熟。没想到是吴宓的亲炙弟子。肃然起敬。

吴宓为人迂阔，固执且懦弱，又情思细密，负了佳人，苦了自己。这种浪漫，运用到翻译情诗，自然得心应手，八面玲珑。他翻译的英国女诗人Rossetti的Remember，运用五言古体意译，如神来之笔。

Remember me when I am gone away,
愿君常忆我，逝矣从兹别

Gone far away into the silent land;
相见及黄泉，渺渺音尘绝

When you can no more hold me by hand,
昔来常欢会，执手深情结

Nor I half turn to go yet turning stay.
临去又回身，千言意犹切

Remember me when no more day by day
絮絮话家常，白首长相契

You tell me of our future that you planned.
此景伤难再，吾生忽易辙

Only remember me , you understand
祝告两无益，寸心已如铁

It will be late to counsel then or pray.
惟期常忆我，从兹成永诀

Yet if you should forget me for a while
君如暂忘我，回思勿自嗔

And afterwards remember, do not grieve;
我愿君愉乐，不愿君苦辛

For if the darkness and corruption leave
我生无邪思，皎洁断纤尘

A vestige of the thoughts that once I had,
留君心上影，忍令失君真

Better by far you should forget and smile
忘时君欢笑，忆时君愁颦

Than that you should remember and be sad.
愿君常忆我，即此语谆谆

英国人和美国人

我是英国文学出身,自然痴迷于英国文化,倾向英式英语。英人清高保守,含蓄内敛。美国佬与人初识,会满面堆笑,大大咧咧,"Hi,我是Jack,来自纽约"。而英国人碰到这样的老美,只尴尬地挤出笑容,紧巴巴地回答,"Hello"?便矜持地保持沉默。美国人等到笑容凝固,未见下文,傻乎乎地很受伤,心里恨恨地骂,连个名字也不告诉我?

同样,中国人初次见面,出于自谦,也很少自报家门,一般由人引见。除非草莽英雄,"燕人张飞张翼德在此,谁是贼兵主帅,还不上来受死"!声如炸雷,豪气盈天。如有名不见经传之鼠辈道,"你好,我是来自纽约的杰克"。便仿佛雄赳赳的一声,"你好,我乃村东头郑屠'镇关西'是也"。

英国人通常不屑知道你名字,除非熟悉程度略有加深,比如你娶了他们的女儿什么的。交换名号,一般等到亲切交谈之后,但不会主动报料或索名,总是等对方采取主动。倘若对方不幸比你更绅士老道,按兵不动,可以说,"Goodbye, nice to meet you."然后做如梦初醒状,"Er...oh, I didn't catch your name"?对方少不得心领神会,做受宠若惊状,道出姓名。最后再不经意地报上自己家门,"I'm David, by the way"。这个by the way要配上脸部轻描淡写状。这一番微妙交锋,心照不宣。天真如美国人者,如何能体会?美国人很可爱,有着捶胸顿足般的真诚。英国人更贴近中国风味的世故狡黠,意味深长。如果能把英国绅士风度和中国士大夫风骨结合起来,应该是21世纪的国际标准。

见美国人悻悻不安，英人优雅地环顾天色，"phew! It's hot，Isn't it"？美国人听了，立刻来了神，手舞足蹈，"哎哟，这也叫热？不算啥。你要知道什么是热，去咱们得克萨斯看看，哎哟那个热呀……"直到英国人脸上浮出鄙夷，老美才讪讪住嘴。

英国人谈天气，和中国人问"吃了吗"一样，不指望否定的回答。所以上面的It's hot. Isn't it? 天真热，是吗？说者无心，听者也该随口答道，"Mmm, very hot."这简单得如同领导说，"同志们好"！我们就得凛然道，"首长好"！，而不能齐声诉苦，"我们不好！缺衣少食，上有80老母，下有黄口小儿……"之类。美国人在历史长河里涉世未深，偏偏喜欢较真，连声说，哎哟哎哟这哪热呀，不热不热真不热。阿甘似的。

若碰上年少毛糙的英国人，也许略有不快。经过一小段尴尬的沉默，会自我解嘲，"Well, it feels hot to me."不和老美一般见识，还把责任揽给了自己。而大多数英国绅士，体贴入微，好似看到做客的懵懂孩童，无意打翻了自家的花瓶，脸上浮出慈祥宽厚的笑容，并努力帮忙打圆场，掩盖美国人的小错。"Oh, er, 也许你不觉得热。和我老婆一样，她特怕冷。这样的天气她觉得正好。嘿嘿，女人总比男人怕冷……呵呵呵，哈哈哈……"

没想到美国人又来了神，正色道，"不不，男人也有怕冷的。我那舅舅约翰，可不咋的……您瞧……呵呵呵，哈哈哈……"

英国人哭笑不得，只得撇撇嘴，准备闪人，还和蔼地说，"Pleased to meet you"。美国佬一怔，受宠若惊，旋又心花怒放起来，"他很高兴见到我"？

为了坠落的飞翔

象牙塔里的跳楼悲剧，层出不穷，麻木了人们的神经。前一阵，网上报道，一位女研究生又选择了绝路。没有沸沸扬扬的舆论。反响寥寥，于逝者，未尝不是好事，寂然离去，免却纷扰。而人们竟至习以为常，就是悲哀了。

读过一首英文诗，日裔美国诗人Janice Mirikitani写的。记忆中的景象苍白冰冷。一个在美求学的日本女大学生，没得到更优秀的成绩，冬夜里从寝室窗口，奋力扑向漆黑僵硬的大地，只为坠落。

诗的名字叫Suicide Note，遗言。

Not good enough　　not pretty enough　　not smart enough
Dear mother and father.
I apologize
For disappointing you.
I have worked very hard,
　　　　　Not good enough
Harder, perhaps to please you.

"我不够优秀／我不够漂亮／我不够聪明…／亲爱的爸爸妈妈／对不起／我让你们失望了／我很努力，很努力，／尽量让你们高兴……"

这首诗以女儿急急的道歉开始,平实里带着紧迫。后面的部分我省略了,女儿因自己不是男孩,而满怀歉意。
—I apologize.
Tasks do not come easily.
Each failure, a glacier.
Each disapproval, a bootprint,
Each disappointment,
Ice above my river.
So I have worked hard.
     Not good enough
"对不起／我做得不好／每一次失败／都是我的冰川纪／每一次拒绝／都是踏在我心口的脚印／每一次失望／都让我的心河覆上层层冰霜／所以,我很努力,很努力／我不够优秀／不够。"一个乖乖女,苦苦挣扎,攀上窗台,迎着风雪泣不成声。雪花狂舞,争先恐后扑向大地,积聚成毡,想承受一位女子的生命之重。它们不懂:为何一念间,成了决绝?
It's snowing steadily
Surely not good weather
For flying–this sparrow
Sillied and dizzied by the wind on the edge.
Not good enough

"大雪沉沉地下／是的,天气不好／不适合飞翔／凄风苦雨中／这只傻傻的小麻雀／站在窗沿／怔忡,恍惚,惶悚……／我不够优秀……"

窗外缤缤纷纷,只为成全一场坠落的飞翔。漫天雪花,寂寂茫茫,每一片都扑向她耳边,说,"sorry, sorry, sorry…"

97

赵承熙枪击案一：心是孤独的猎手

2007年4月16日上午9点左右。美国弗吉尼亚理工大学，工程系教学楼。赵承熙推开207教室的门，探头张望，退了出去。基础德语课的同学并没在意，以为他走错了教室。赵承熙又同样去了206和204。9点半左右，他回到206教室。高级水利学研究生课程正在进行。他举枪便射，G.V.Loganathan教授应声倒地。赵承熙转过身，美国历史上最严重的校园枪击案惨烈上演。事后，幸存者回忆，赵承熙是在寻找人多的教室，以便射杀更多的人，用最短的时间。像一名沉着的猎手。

《心是孤独的猎手》，美国作家Carson McCullers的小说。读研时，我在图书馆漫无目的地逡巡，从满满一书架逛到另一书架，突然被这本书名吸引：The Heart Is a Lonely Hunter。孤独落寞，浸透纸背。

这是小镇上两个聋哑人的故事。其中一个胖的是智障，被送进精神病院。另一个瘦的，叫辛格，变得更加孤僻。沉默幽深的他，却成了小镇人的倾诉对象。人们在分裂的世界里独自挣扎，彼此隔膜，却把交流的渴望托付给一个身处无声世界的聋哑人。而辛格自己的孤独，只能在那个傻傻胖胖的神经哑巴面前，用手舞足蹈，激情热烈的手语化解。胖哑巴死后，辛格的精神支柱轰然坍塌，举枪自杀。小镇上的人们，继续揣着无所依附的心，茫然游走，期望猎取理解和交流。

在我眼里，赵承熙仿佛一缕孤魂，从这本书中飘散出来，化为沉默、仇恨、爆发和灭亡。我读了这几天的《纽约时报》。小时侯，赵承熙就曾被亲戚认为是哑巴，或精神有问题。他的悲哀，其实甚于聋哑人。他身处有声世界，却无言以对。像一名乐手，端着一把喑哑的小提琴，站在舞台上，却置身一场协奏合奏之外。唯有用枪声，奏响一场决绝独奏。

赵承熙可能从小就患有自闭症，或失语症。8岁随父母移居美国。母亲以为美国开放的环境能缓解他的孤独。家里生活贫困，开了一家干洗店。大华盛顿地区2000多家干洗店，有1800家属于韩国人。这是最不需要用英语交流的行业。我看到小赵承熙默默蹲在干洗店门前。眼前的情景日复一日，年复一年。一手交钱，一手交货，无声无息。人们表情僵硬，匆匆来去。那个洗衣店门前的小男孩，仿佛从没存在过。

中学时，赵承熙英文粗糙，性格孤僻，遭人嘲笑，备受欺凌。成绩不佳，在韩国社区里，是奇耻大辱。和中国社区一样，这里各类SAT等培优班星罗棋布。常春藤名校令每个父母魂牵梦萦。当地的韩文报纸，时常公布考取名校的状元名单，以励后生。赵承熙的姐姐，报考普林思顿，榜上有名。赵承熙彷徨无助，局促不安。他的外部空间，日益狭小，处处催逼。

我感觉，赵承熙在学业上付出过巨大心血，显示出勤奋的一面。从英文受人嘲笑，到成为英文专业的学生，其间的努力和挣扎，难以想象。我看到他在录像带里，用词精确，陈述清晰，甚至辞藻考究。

"You had a hundred billion chances and ways to have avoided today ... Now you have blood on your hands that will never wash off."

"You just loved to crucify me. You loved inducing cancer in my head, terror in my heart, ripping my soul."

"Your Mercedes wasn't enough, you brats. Your golden necklaces weren't enough, you snobs. Your trust fund ... your vodka and cognac wasn't enough. All your debaucheries weren't enough ... to fulfil your hedonistic needs."

字字仇恨，句句狰狞，声声泣血。在沉默中爆发，又在爆发中灭亡。

《心是孤独的猎手》里，辛格身边的人，寄居在他的沉默里，渴求交流。辛格生前，只是安静地浅笑着回应人们的各类诉说和信任。他听不见，更听不懂他们的孤独。他空空茫茫的眼睛里，只有那个傻胖子痴痴的笑。傻子死了，连辛格都孤独了，追随而去，人们就散了。

赵承熙枪击案二：更多的人死于心碎

美国枪击案，屡见不绝。反响最大的，莫过于弗吉尼亚理工学院的赵承熙枪击案。当时我在《纽约时报》上，见到其奶奶的照片。老人伤心欲绝。此案受害者数十名，而更多的人，父母，姐妹，师长，同学，死难者亲友，同胞，却死于心碎。

很多年前，读了Herzog以后，我开始痴迷Saul Bellow的作品。《更多的人死于心碎》，是他的一部后期小说，内容早已忘却，小说名却一直记忆犹新。看到那张照片，脑海里突然闪过这句话，more die of a heartbreak。

最伤心者，莫过于家人。赵承熙的父亲家境贫寒，母亲出身于朝鲜农民家庭，朝鲜战争后逃难而来。父亲在沙特做过石油和建筑劳工。1984年应在美亲戚邀请，准备赴美发展，改善家人生活。8年后才拿到签证。在美国开了家干洗店，做熨衣工，劳碌至今。

赵承熙从小自闭，陌生环境下，内心的城墙日趋坚厚。他抬起头，辛勤劳作的父亲，伛偻苍老，无语蹒跚。"哧……"的一声，有熨斗蒸汽弥散开来，小男孩眼前一片模糊，一团又一团的云雾升腾起来，在脑海里左冲右撞，没有出路。

勤劳的父母，像所有东方人一样，对孩子倾注了全部希望。赵承熙听话懂事，却沉默寡言，成了母亲的一块心病。"From the beginning, he did not talk. Not to other children, not to his own family… Talk, she just wanted him to talk."（《纽约时报》）同龄的孩子们，唧唧喳喳，活泼好动。而母亲对他的最大期望是：说话。"说话，请张嘴说话，我的孩子。"母亲苦苦哀求，小男孩倔强缄默的眼神，令家人心碎欲裂。

赵承熙的姐姐赵善庆曾发表声明致歉。她说，"赵承熙使整个世界哭泣，我们仿佛身处噩梦之中。我们一家对我弟弟制造的可怕事件深感抱歉。对我们来说，这同样也是一个可怕的悲剧"。姐姐出面致歉，意味着两位老人的无力承担，心力交瘁和精神崩溃。他们如何面对32位死者家人的心碎？有细细密密的裂纹，慢慢蔓延，如暗夜里枝枝桠桠的闪电般惊悚，让更多的人死于心碎。

"自闭的世界里，有种上不着天下不着地的寂寞。抑郁的孩子也渴望靠近阳光。"《长江商报》的"心理说吧"曾登载了一位自闭的武汉女孩，李安安，15岁，性格温和，喜欢画画。10岁患上轻度抑郁，并带有自闭情结。和赵承熙一样，她并不像天生自闭症的孩子，放弃任何交流。依然听话地上学、读书。她的眼睛清澈明亮，但眼神发散迷茫。

如今自闭症儿童越来越多。生活、工作节奏加快，父母只管吃穿，无暇顾及子女的情感。网络的发展，提供虚拟世界，隔绝了孩子与外界的交流。商品房鳞次栉比，人们的单位意识消失。孩子的世界，陌生隔膜，提防敌视。我小时候，整院子小朋友吆五喝六，呼啸成群。这种盛况不复存在。只剩下怯生生的眼神，在阳台上，在门背后躲躲闪闪。

《长江商报》的记者王晴写道，

"古龙小说里小李飞刀对自己的好朋友阿飞说，树上的桃花开了19朵。阿飞惊讶地想，连树上桃花开了几朵都知道的人该有多寂寞啊。我见到李安安，她跟我说的第一句话就是，姐姐，树上的树叶已经飘下了23片……

明亮的房间，无颜六色的水彩，洁白的画纸，一个安静的女孩，窗外落下一片树叶，女孩慢慢地抬头……像一个脱离尘世的世界……"

我想起了另外一个问题。20年来，中国的计划生育政策，对控制人口，成效卓著，但负面效应渐渐凸显。李工真教授曾说过："人类历史上从未出现过的现象正在中国上演：一个几千万人的群体茕茕独立，他们没有兄弟姐妹。"这群人没有经历过兄长的模范和谦让，弟弟的服从和尊长，姐姐的关爱和细心，妹妹的忍耐和等待。没有和同年龄段孩子朝夕相处的经验，会造成性格塑造和交际能力的缺失。没有正确的引导和教育，会趋向自闭、孤独和偏执。

20世纪70年代末出生的第一代独生子女，部分引发了一轮离婚热潮。这一代人，其实还在孝悌的传统下长大，健康向上，并没有体现出独生子女的负面社会效应。但他们绝大多数已进入生育高峰，试想，独生子女的独生子女，承担的是21世纪民族中兴的重任。如果没有必要的、外在的社会以及内在的家庭教育手段，进行心理调适和行为指导，会出现什么后果？再后面一代呢？我们难道要眼睁睁看着自闭、偏执、孤独，淡漠融入中华种族的基因里，形成物种的缺陷，导致最终的灭绝吗？

70年前对失利奥运健儿的鼓励

我藏有一本1937年出版的英文《少年中国论文》（*Essays for Young China*，似乎应译为《少年中国论说》），作者谢颂羔，一位民国期间基督教广学会的牧师，曾翻译过很多英文作品。在《少年中国论说》里，谢牧师用浅显英文讲述中国的一切，爱国之心溢于言表。

书里有一篇文章，What the Olympic games taught me? 关于1936年柏林奥运之后的感触。1936年的中国，山河破碎，有69名运动员参加了柏林奥运。因经费缺乏，经受了一个月海上颠簸的中国运动员，精疲力竭，大多止步于预赛和及格线外，铩羽而归。

谢牧师的文章语气沉痛，却不乏鼓励、祝福与期待。我摘录第一段和最后一段，以供英语爱好者学习，并附上中文大意：

The 1936 Olympics games were held in Berlin, Germany. Germany came in first, and the USA second. The shame was China's, because she came nowhere, not even receiving a brass medal. (1936年奥运会在柏林举行。德国第一，美国第二。中国名落孙山，蒙受耻辱，连一枚铜牌都无缘。)

Now a word of encouragement for the defeated athletes. You have faced defeat in Berlin: now let that fact be cast aside. Forget publicity and fame, but work hard, harder than ever before. (今向失利健儿作一鼓励之语。请抛开失败，忘却功名，发奋图强。)Show the world that you can win your game. At the next Olympic Games, there are many golden medals waiting for you...Don't be discouraged, but face the issue calmly and confidently, give the best that is in you, and prove to the world that Chinese boys and girls can run faster than boys and girls of other nations. The glory is yet to come.(展现给世界你们能赢罢。下一次奥运，金牌虚位以待！不要气馁，正视现状，尽君之力，向世界证明中华健儿跑得更快。辉煌尚在将来!)

谢牧师无从知道，他翘首以待的"下一次"，也就是1940年奥运，将在战火纷飞中化为泡影。他发表文章的时候，日寇的铁蹄已踏破华北大地，山河变色。一年后，南京屠杀惨绝人寰，祖国一片焦土，生灵涂炭。

更残酷的是，1940年原本定为东京奥运会，后遭抵制，最终因"二战"硝烟不了了之。中华健儿报国无门，空负了谢牧师一腔热诚。

读到这里，刘翔的矫健身姿倏地从脑海掠过。那冲向终点的纵身一跃，让谢牧师等了70多年，还未能亲见。突然觉得，自己对现实的种种不快，都卑微琐屑，不足挂齿。这个时代的我们，真的很幸福。